# New Crafts
# CARDBOARD

# New Crafts
# CARDBOARD
## Emma Hardy

### PHOTOGRAPHY BY PETER WILLIAMS

LORENZ BOOKS

LONDON • NEW YORK • SYDNEY • BATH

*For Laurie and Anna*

THIS EDITION FIRST PUBLISHED IN THE UK IN 1997
BY LORENZ BOOKS

LORENZ BOOKS IS AN IMPRINT OF
ANNESS PUBLISHING LIMITED
HERMES HOUSE
88–89 BLACKFRIARS ROAD
LONDON SE1 8HA

THIS EDITION DISTRIBUTED IN CANADA BY
RAINCOAST BOOKS DISTRIBUTION LIMITED, VANCOUVER

© 1997 ANNESS PUBLISHING LIMITED

ISBN 1 85967 532 8

A CIP CATALOGUE RECORD FOR THIS BOOK IS AVAILABLE
FROM THE BRITISH LIBRARY

PUBLISHER: JOANNA LORENZ
SENIOR EDITOR: CLARE NICHOLSON
DESIGNER: ROGER WALKER
PHOTOGRAPHER: PETER WILLIAMS
STYLIST: GEORGINA RHODES
ILLUSTRATOR: MADELEINE DAVID

PRINTED AND BOUND IN HONG KONG

10 9 8 7 6 5 4 3 2 1

# CONTENTS

# INTRODUCTION

Few people, when they see cardboard in use as an everyday packing and carrying material, realize how versatile and exciting a craft material it can be. In this book each project has been carefully designed to be fully functional, creating stunning but durable pieces from next to nothing. The book will enable you to create your own cardboard constructions by following the step-by-step instructions for each project. The Basic Techniques section explains the different ways of working with the cardboard used in the projects. The Gallery shows a range of cardboard structures made by artists and sold in retail outlets, and aims to inspire you to develop works of your own design.

*Left: Cardboard can be used to make a wide range of functional and decorative items.*

# HISTORY OF CARDBOARD

CARDBOARD HAS BEEN USED FOR OVER A HUNDRED YEARS PRIMARILY AS A PACKAGING MATERIAL. IT IS A VERY BASIC PRODUCT THAT WAS ORIGINALLY MADE FROM ROUGH WOOD PULP THAT CREATED QUITE A RAW FINISH. DESPITE ITS BLANDNESS, IT HAS BEEN EMPLOYED BY A NUMBER OF ARTISTS, DESIGNERS AND ARCHITECTS THROUGH THE DECADES. THE QUALITIES OF THE MATERIAL AND ITS AVAILABILITY AND CHEAPNESS HAVE MADE IT AN APPEALING MEDIUM TO MANY AND IT HAS BEEN USED FOR A DIVERSE RANGE OF PROJECTS.

Used mainly in the initial stages of sculpture, furniture and architectural design for mock-ups and model making, cardboard has also been used as the final product. One of the earliest noted designers to use cardboard was the Dutch furniture designer Gerrit Rietveld. In the 1920s he designed pieces that employed basic origami principles and created chairs made from single pieces of cardboard cut and folded in specific ways.

Using cardboard in a creative way became especially popular during the Second World War when resources were low. Cardboard was being used more and more as packaging for food and household goods, including ration and gas-mask boxes. Packaging was simple with very little printing on it and so it became a suitable material to use for crafts. Although it starts its life as a robust material, it becomes more fragile with time and

because of this and the fact that it was often considered a waste material, very few examples of cardboard crafts have survived. There are, however, examples of playing cards made from cardboard cigarette boxes and food packaging boxes, with the suits hand drawn on to them, made by prisoners of war.

The real growth in cardboard production started after the war when corrugated cardboard, made by combining outer layers

*Above: A Christmas crib from Poland that is beautifully crafted out of cardboard.*

known as liners and fluting papers in a liner-fluting-liner sandwich, became widely used. With this basic principle, a wide range of permutations could be created. By using different types of trees and varying the amounts of each ingredient used, many different cardboards could be made. As resources became available after the war, so the use of cardboard in crafts declined.

More recently, cardboard has become recognized as an acceptable material to create with. Designers in the 1960s started to explore the possibilities of cardboard but probably the most well known is Frank

Gehry, an American architect who designed several pieces of cardboard furniture in the early 1980s. His "Easy Edge" chair, made from layers of cardboard laminated together, reinforced the reputation of his work for using materials despised and often not considered by fellow architects.

In the early 1980s a range of cardboard furniture was made for use in prisons. Although initially thought of as a safe and practical idea, with pieces that would not cause damage when thrown, the fire risk was thought to be too great and the furniture did not go into production.

Cardboard has, however, been used in upholstered furniture and is even available in coffin form that is now accepted by most crematoriums, making a very cheap and economical alternative to wood.

Recycling has become more and more of an issue in the last few years and the paper and cardboard industry has been recovering and re-using waste for years.

As well as being made from recycled materials – it is generally made from about 60% recycled pulp – cardboard can be transformed and recycled into craft projects when its original use has come to an end.

*Right: This basket is woven from cigarette packets. It was probably made in the 1940s or 1950s, when other materials were in short supply.*

*Opposite: This patchwork-look laundry basket and waste paper bin are made from food packaging boxes using a traditional plaiting technique, popular around the world, to weave flat materials together. Packing tape is used to bind around the edge of the bin and the top of the laundry basket, and a piece of carved wood is used as a handle. The basket was made by Lois Walpole who is well known for her work using cardboard.*

# GALLERY

THE USE OF CARDBOARD IN A CREATIVE WAY HAS INCREASED ENORMOUSLY OVER RECENT YEARS. AT A TIME WHEN RE-CYCLING IS BECOMING MORE AND MORE IMPORTANT, MANY ARTISTS AND DESIGNERS ARE USING IT IN THEIR WORK. HERE IS A SELECTION OF SOME OF THE PEOPLE WHO ARE WORKING IN CARDBOARD AND SOME ITEMS MADE OUT OF CARDBOARD THAT CAN BE BOUGHT IN SHOPS TODAY. THE DIVERSE RANGE OF STYLES ILLUSTRATES THE NUMBER OF WAYS IN WHICH THE MATERIAL CAN BE USED.

*Right:* COIL POTS
These coil pots are made from one long continuous strip of cardboard (food packaging boxes are used). The strip is rolled up into a coil and the outside edge is pulled up and out, to form a bowl shape. The cardboard is then carefully glued in place and covered with layers of papier mâché. Their lovely, slightly irregular quality adds to the pots' delicate look.
SARAH DREW

*Left:* CARTOON SHOW
This fantastic television is made predominantly from corrugated cardboard. Pieces of broken audio cassette and plastic debris have been used as additional decoration.
DAVID COX

*Above:* BOWL
This bowl is made from strips of unprinted packaging boxes using a twill plaiting technique. The rim of the bowl is made from brown willow, which is flexible and strong. This is stitched on with tarred string, in keeping with the natural look of the piece. The underside of the bowl has been given a paint wash and the cardboard is coated with a polyurethane varnish to make it more durable.
POLLY POLLOCK

*Left and below:* FURNITURE
The Elevated Throne (left) and Chaise Longue (below) are made from rolling, stitching and weaving cardboard to create these splendid pieces of furniture. The designer uses packing cardboard and cardboard tubes as the basis for the pieces, and water-based glue and thick parcel tape to stitch them together. The cushion effect is made from parcel paper which is painted and then the whole piece is sealed with PVA glue.
NIGEL WESTWOOD

*Left:* JAPANESE CARDBOARD ITEMS
These pieces make good use of the utilitarian look of plain cardboard. Muji produce a range of simple, well-designed accessories made from cardboard for the home. The drawers are made from single wall corrugated cardboard using a folding technique to create a very durable, practical storage idea. The round waste paper bin is made from a piece of curved corrugated cardboard held in place with plastic loops at the top and bottom. The fine flute corrugated gift bag is tied with plain cord in keeping with the overall style.
MUJI

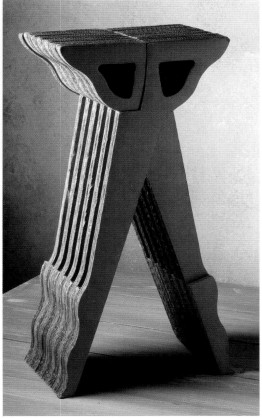

*Right:* STOOL
The inspiration behind this ingenious stool was the traditional Japanese head rest, but the basic principles have been given a modern interpretation. The cardboard has been used in such a way as to maximize its strength, and the stool folds up so that it can be stored easily. The individual pieces that make up the stool are die-cut by a cardboard box manufacturer and each layer is glued together to create a very stylish piece of furniture.
TOMOKO AZUMI

*Left:* TOY BASKET

Strips of cardboard have been woven together to make this toy or linen basket using a straight plaiting or check weave technique. The cardboard is first painted in a colourful abstract pattern, using PVA paints, before being cut into strips. Thin plastic tubing is used to bind around the top of the basket and a ledge is stuck inside to hold the drop-in lid in place.

POLLY POLLOCK

*Above:* HANDBAG

Made from strips of crisp packet boxes, this charming handbag makes use of the traditional bias plaiting method of weaving. A plastic handle and toggle have been used to make it more practical. Although this particular example has been left in its natural state, it could be coated with a flexible varnish like polyurethane or acrylic for extra protection.

POLLY POLLOCK

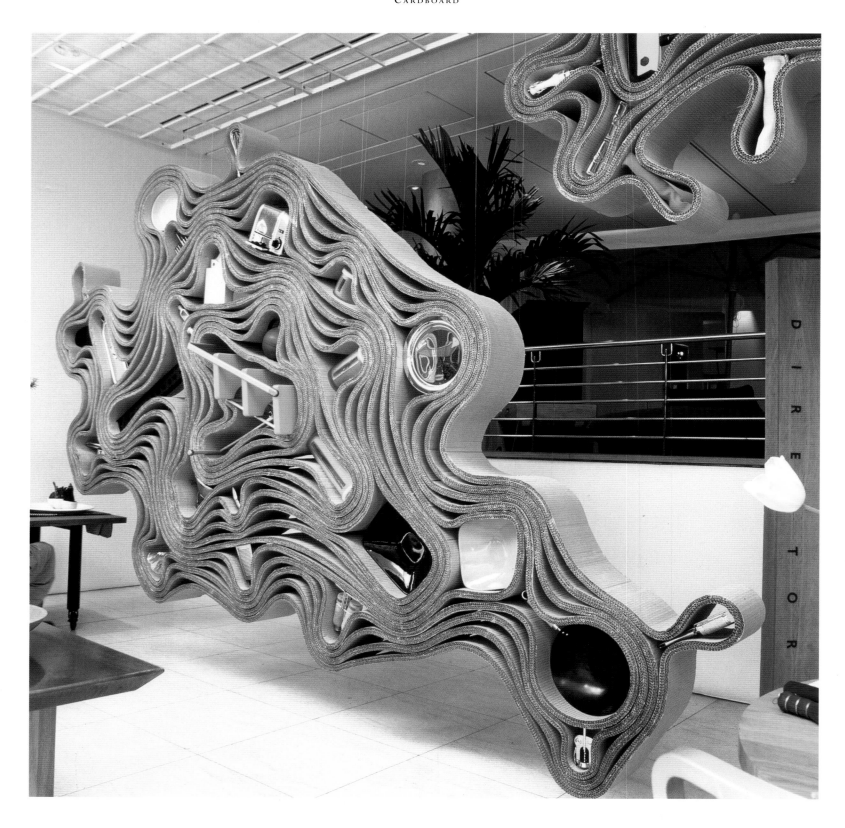

*Opposite:*
WINDOW
DISPLAY
This cleverly
constructed
window installation
for the Conran Shop
is an ingenious way
to display products.
It was made on the
ground from layers
of single-faced
corrugated
cardboard (about
4.5km / 2¾ miles
was used in total)
curved around the
products and glued
with hot glue. It was
then lifted up and
suspended from the
ceiling using thin
nylon thread pinned
through the
cardboard.
THOMAS
HEATHERWICK
(PHOTOGRAPH BY
MATTHEW MAY)

*Right:* ADDRESS
BOOKS
Carton Massif
design a range of
beautiful furniture
and accessories all
made from card-
board. These ele-
gant address books
are made with
cardboard con-
structed to look
like panelling, then
painted in a range
of colours. They
are an excellent
example of how
plain cardboard
can be used to
create exquisite
pieces of work.
CARTON MASSIF

# EQUIPMENT

MOST OF THE PIECES OF EQUIPMENT NEEDED FOR MAKING THE PROJECTS IN THIS BOOK ARE STANDARD HOUSEHOLD ITEMS. PROBABLY THE MOST IMPORTANT TOOL IS SOMETHING TO SCORE THE CARDBOARD WITH — THE BACK OF A WOODEN SPOON IS IDEAL. SOME OF THE PROJECTS REQUIRE MORE SPECIALIST TOOLS BUT MOST OF THEM ARE OPTIONAL.

**Bradawl** A bradawl is a useful tool for making small holes in cardboard (see Christmas tree decorations). It is suitable for using on most cardboards apart from single-faced corrugated boards which will tend to rip.

**Clothes pegs** are extremely useful for holding cardboard together while waiting for it to dry. They are also used to hold the woven basket while weaving the strips of cardboard together.

**Craft knives** are needed for most of the projects. A small craft knife with disposable blades is ideal so that the blade can be replaced when blunt. A heavier-weight knife is needed to cut through thick card. Scalpels with small sharp points are also useful for cutting into small areas (see doll's house). Always keep the blade sharp to avoid ripping the card when cutting.

**Cutting mat** Although quite expensive, it is worth investing in a good self-sealing cutting mat — the larger the better. The mat can be used time and again and will still have a smooth non-slip surface that makes cutting much easier.

**Hammer** A hammer is needed when joining metal eyelets together and making the basic wooden frame for the pelmet project.

**Heavy-duty stapler** A general household stapler is fine when joining lightweight card, but when several thicknesses of corrugated card are being secured together a heavy-duty stapler is needed.

**Paintbrush** A paintbrush is required for several of the projects. Use a soft-haired brush when painting corrugated cardboard so that the bristles can gently get into difficult corners.

**Pair of compasses** Compasses are needed for drawing accurate circles and they have the added advantage that they mark the centre of the circle, which is useful if the circle has to be divided up accurately. A sharp pencil is preferable to a pen.

**Revolving hole punch** is a useful tool for making neat holes in cardboard. It usually has six settings varying from about 2 mm/$\frac{1}{16}$ in wide to 5 mm/$\frac{1}{4}$ in wide and is easy to use.

**Rulers** Most of the projects require a ruler for measuring and also cutting. Wooden rulers are suitable for measuring accurately, but always use a metal ruler for cutting. Heavier-weight rulers with a rubber base are useful when cutting very thick card as they do not slip.

**Saws** are needed for several of the projects in the book. A general-purpose saw is needed for cutting the wood for the pelmet and a smaller hacksaw is needed for cutting the overflow tank coupler when making the card table.

**Scissors** in various sizes are handy when using single-faced board (packing card) which can easily rip when cut with a craft knife. Small embroidery scissors are used when making the fringing for the pelmet as the blades are small enough not to cut right through the strips of cardboard. Cutting cardboard will blunt scissors quite quickly so have them sharpened regularly.

**Wire cutters** are needed to cut the wire for the chandelier. The wire is quite easy to cut and so lightweight wire cutters or general-purpose pliers will do the job well.

**Wooden spoon** A wooden spoon with a pointed end is a useful implement for scoring single and double wall cardboard because it flattens the flutes without ripping the surface of the cardboard. Any object with a blunt point will work well.

KEY

| | |
|---|---|
| **1** Bradawl | **8** Pair of compasses |
| **2** Clothes pegs | **9** Rulers |
| **3** Craft knives | **10** Saws |
| **4** Cutting mat | **11** Scissors |
| **5** Hammer | **12** Wire cutters |
| **6** Heavy-duty stapler | **13** Wooden spoon |
| **7** Paintbrush | **14** Revolving hole punch |

# MATERIALS

THE PROJECTS IN THIS BOOK ARE MADE PRINCIPALLY OUT OF CARDBOARD, WITH A FEW USING PAINTS FOR DECORATION. IN ADDITION TO THE CARDBOARD, THE MOST IMPORTANT MATERIALS ARE THE DIFFERENT GLUES AND CLIPS TO HOLD THE CARD TOGETHER. IF MORE SPECIALIST MATERIALS ARE REQUIRED, THESE ARE LISTED IN THE INDIVIDUAL PROJECTS.

## CARDBOARDS

Corrugated cardboard is made from outer layers called liners. These are usually made from either unbleached kraft (German for strong) paper (made from a high proportion of pure wood pulp) or testliners (made from recycled waste with additives, such as starch to give strength, and dyed brown) and fluting papers, which are either water-based or semi-chemical made from hardwood pulp.

The thickness of cardboard is measured by its fluting. The fluting profile refers to the height and width of the fluting between the liners. They range from E type (height 1.2 mm / $\frac{1}{20}$ in and width 3.25 mm / $\frac{1}{7}$ in) to A type (height 4.7 mm / $\frac{1}{5}$ in and width 8.5 mm / $\frac{1}{3}$ in). The cardboards used in the projects in this

book have been described in more general terms, either fine, medium or large fluting — the exact fluting size can be varied, apart from the card table and child's chair, which require the thickest cardboard available.

For the projects which require flat cardboard, think of the qualities needed for that item (whether it should be flexible, strong etc) when deciding what type to use.

**Single wall corrugated cardboard** is made from two layers of unbleached kraft paper with medium fluting laminated between them. It is generally used for dry food packaging and is strong and durable.
**Single wall corrugated cardboard with a printed surface** This is made into

fruit boxes and again is strong and durable. (Both these types can be found in markets and supermarkets and are therefore extremely economical to use for craft projects.)
**Single wall corrugated cardboard with a smooth brown surface** The fluting is medium which makes for a tough, robust cardboard with a neat finish.
**Lower-grade single wall corrugated cardboard** has similar qualities to the above but a slightly rougher look.
**Double wall corrugated cardboard** consists of an outer, inner and central liner, used to separate two layers of fluting paper. The fluting papers are usually different flute sizes from each other to increase the strength of the cardboard.

KEY

1 Single wall corrugated board
2 Single wall corrugated board with a printed surface
3 Single wall corrugated board with a smooth brown surface
4 Lower-grade single wall corrugated cardboard
5 Double wall corrugated cardboard
6 Artist's mounting board
7 Double thickness unlined chipboard
8 Bleached cardboard
9 Manila card
10 Thin unlined chipboard
11 Recycled newspaper board
12 Unlined chipboard
13 Polyboard
14 Single-faced corrugated cardboard

15 + 17 Very fine single-faced corrugated cardboard with fine fluting
16 + 18 Medium fluted single-faced corrugated board

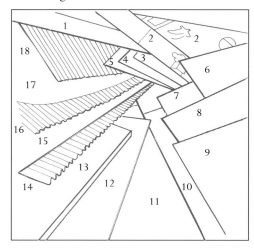

**Artist's mounting board** is a strong, inflexible board used to mount photographs and paintings. The board is usually white with a layer of coloured paper laminated to one side. It is available in a wide selection of colours and is smooth on the back with a slightly fibrous texture on the coloured side.

**Bleached cardboard** is very flexible and has a slightly glazed surface. It is ideal for projects which need to be strong but are curved or shaped. It has a very smooth finish which can be painted or covered in paper.

**Manila card** has a lovely quality when it is left in its natural state, and makes an ideal material for greetings cards because it folds neatly. It is also available as oiled manila having been treated with linseed oil, which gives it a slightly mottled finish. This is generally used as stencil card but makes a very appealing material for craft projects such as the lampshades.

**Unlined chipboard** is available in different weights. The thicker version is a very basic board with a slightly rough surface which is suitable for a variety of storage and box-making projects. The thicker the card, the less flexible it will be.

**Double thickness unlined chipboard** is basically two sheets of chipboard stuck together to produce a tough, smooth-sided board. Available in its basic grey form, it can be easily painted and is suitable for straight-sided projects. It will need to be cut with a heavy-duty knife with a very sharp blade.

**Thin unlined chipboard** is a very basic board which is used for simple packaging. It is slightly flexible but bends and creases easily and is not particularly strong because it is made from a mixture of low-grade pulp.

**Recycled newspaper board** is specifically made for its decorative qualities and has similar qualities to the board above but is slightly more flexible. The flecks of newspaper are in keeping with the basic look of the board but add a more interesting finish.

**Polyboard** is made from two layers of very smooth bleached card laminated over a layer of polystyrene. It is quite strong and it cannot be folded and should be glued or pinned together.

**Single-faced corrugated cardboard** is usually made from a layer of chip paper or unbleached kraft paper with a wide fluted layer laminated to it. This is a general-purpose, very cheap corrugate which is used for packaging. It is used in several of the projects in this book and can be bought in very large quantities from packaging suppliers or in small rolls from stationers and craft shops.

**Very fine single-faced corrugated cardboard with fine fluting** has very similar qualities to single-faced corrugated cardboard, but has a much smarter, more finished look. It is very flexible and easy to cut and available in an array of bright colours as well as natural brown and grey.

**Medium flute single-faced corrugated cardboard** is available in several colours, as well as in metallic finishes, and is slightly less flexible than the single-faced boards because the flat cardboard used is slightly thicker.

### GLUES AND PAINTS

Rubber solution glue is a spreadable glue which should be applied to both surfaces and left to dry before bonding. It has high adhesive qualities and excess glue can be removed easily by rubbing it off with your finger.

Water-based, high-tack, fast-drying glue is an excellent all-purpose glue that is ideal for sticking lighter-weight cardboards together. Because it dries quickly, it is ideal when making things which have to be held in place while drying.

Rubber solution and PVA-mix glue is easy to spread and gives a strong bond, but takes a while to dry thoroughly. It is therefore only suitable for projects which do not have to be held together while drying.

Spray adhesive is useful for sticking cardboard sheets together that may need repositioning. It is used for sticking two sheets together for the waste paper bin project. When the cardboard is curved to make the bin, the two layers may need to be repositioned slightly so that they bend together.

Wood glue is used on the wooden pelmet base and is also a good glue to use for heavy-duty projects that need a strong bond.

Masking tape is a good tape to use on cardboard because it can be removed without ripping the card. Use a low-tack tape and test it on a piece of spare cardboard first.

Spray paint can be used on any cardboard and is an effective way of colouring it evenly. Available from craft and DIY shops in a wide selection of colours, as well as metallics, it should always be used in a well-ventilated space. Car spray paints can also be used. Alternatively, water-based paints give a good matt colour on cardboard.

*Above, clockwise from bottom left: rubber solution, wood glue, strong glue, PVA glue, spray paint, spray adhesive and masking tape.*

# BASIC TECHNIQUES

CARDBOARD IS A VERY EASY MATERIAL TO HANDLE AND DOES NOT REQUIRE MANY SPECIALIST SKILLS. THE FOLLOWING ARE A FEW OF THE BASIC TECHNIQUES THAT ARE NEEDED FOR MAKING THE PROJECTS IN THIS BOOK. LOOK THROUGH THIS SECTION BEFORE STARTING THE PROJECTS AND REFER BACK TO IT FOR ADDITIONAL INFORMATION.

### SCORING FINE CARDBOARD

This crops up in several of the projects. To bend cardboard neatly, it needs to be scored first. Always score the smooth side of corrugated cardboard or the flutes will break and look ugly. To score fine cardboard press the blade of a craft knife, using a metal ruler, along the fold line, being careful not to cut into too much of the surface. Then gently fold the cardboard with the scored line inside the fold so that the outside of the fold is smooth.

### SCORING ACROSS THE FLUTES ON THICK CARDBOARD

To get a neat fold on thick corrugated cardboard, use a wooden spoon with a blunt point on it or a blunt pastry wheel. Run the point of the spoon along the fold line, using a ruler as a guide. Try not to rip the surface of the cardboard; you should be just flattening the flutes.

### SCORING ALONG THE FLUTES ON THICK CARDBOARD

If the score line runs along the flutes of the cardboard, just run the edge of your thumb between the flutes firmly to make an indent. Do not use your nail as this may rip the surface.

### FOLDING THICK CARDBOARD

To fold thick corrugated cardboard along the scored line, hold a ruler to one side of the line firmly. Carefully push the cardboard up along the other side of the line. Hold the cardboard with the flat of your hand so that it does not bend in the wrong place.

### MAKING HOLES

Use a revolving hole punch to make neat holes in the cardboard. Mark the position of the hole and, having chosen the required setting, squeeze the punch together firmly on the mark, twisting it slightly so that the hole will be cut properly.

## MAKING CURVED SHAPES

To make curved shapes, for the arms of the child's chair and panels of the screen for instance, simply mark where the curve is to be and, choosing a paint can, cup or plate of the right size, draw around a section of it on to the cardboard.

## STRENGTHENING CARDBOARD

To strengthen corrugated cardboard further, sandwich several layers together with the flutes running vertically and horizontally to each other, so maximizing the strength of each layer. Use a strong glue and leave to dry completely before cutting.

## PEELING OFF THE LINING PAPER

Some of the projects require single wall corrugated cardboard to be bent, and to do this one of the liners needs to be removed. Sometimes this can be quite simply pulled off, but if the cardboard is tough the liner needs to be cut first.

1 With a sharp craft knife, cut slits along the flutes of the cardboard, making sure that you do not cut into the other side.

2 Carefully peel away the strips of cardboard and discard them. Remove any small pieces of the liner that are still attached. The cardboard will now bend easily.

## CURVING CARDBOARD

To curve cardboard, hold the edge of it with the palm of your hand and apply a little pressure until it bends slightly. Keep the pressure on until the cardboard will stay slightly bent when the pressure is removed.

## JOINING CARDBOARD STRIPS TOGETHER

To join strips of cardboard together, cut away a small section of lining paper and fluting on the end of one strip, leaving just one layer of lining paper attached. Apply glue to this and stick the end of the other strip on top, butting up the ends.

# GREETINGS CARDS AND GIFT TAGS

Homemade greetings cards are to be kept and treasured and make a lovely gift. These stylish cards and gift tags make good use of the natural look of fine corrugated cardboard, with thin manila cardboard and natural raffia adding the finishing touches. Choose one of these motifs or design your own for an even more personal approach. You could make envelopes from large squares of brown parcel paper with the corners folded into the middle and secured with sealing wax. Use them for wrapping up presents, tying them with lengths of raffia to match the gift tags.

**1** Trace the templates from the back of the book, enlarging to the required size, and transfer on to plain paper. Cut out the shapes and punch holes where indicated with the revolving hole punch using the smallest hole size setting.

**3** Cut out the shapes from the corrugated cardboard with scissors. Punch holes where indicated, again using the hole punch on its smallest setting.

**5** Cut out large rectangles of manila and natural coloured card, fold them exactly in half and stick the embroidered motifs in the centre. Cut out smaller squares and rectangles of card and punch a small hole in each one for the gift tags. Stick more embroidered motifs on to them.

**2** Place the cut-out paper shapes on to the smooth side of the corrugated cardboard and carefully draw around them with a pencil. Mark the positions of all the holes making sure that the template does not move.

**4** Cut a length of raffia and thread it through the darning needle. Stitch the shapes with the raffia using the photograph as a guide. Finish off the stitching with a small knot on the back of each shape.

**6** For each gift tag, cut a length of raffia and fold in half to make a loop. Thread the loop through the hole, pass the ends through the loop and pull.

## MATERIALS AND EQUIPMENT YOU WILL NEED

TRACING PAPER • PENCIL • PLAIN PAPER • SCISSORS • REVOLVING HOLE PUNCH • VERY FINE SINGLE-FACED CORRUGATED CARDBOARD •
NATURAL RAFFIA • LARGE DARNING NEEDLE • MANILA AND NATURAL COLOURED CARD • HIGH-TACK GLUE

# TABLE LAMP

CREATE AN UNUSUAL AND STYLISH TABLE LAMP BY BINDING TOGETHER RECTANGLES OF THICK, PLAIN GREY CHIPBOARD WITH SMALL KNOTS OF STRING. THE SHADE IS DESIGNED TO SIT OVER THE LAMP FITTING AND WILL CAST A WARM GLOW. MAKE SEVERAL SHADES IN DIFFERENT SIZES AND USE THEM OVER OUTDOOR NIGHT-LIGHTS FOR A SUMMER GARDEN PARTY TO LIGHT UP A PATH. PUNCH SMALL HOLES FROM THE CHIPBOARD PANELS SO THAT THE LIGHT WILL SHINE THROUGH. IF YOU ARE GOING TO USE THE SHADE OVER NIGHT-LIGHTS OR CANDLES, SPRAY THE BOARD WITH NON-FLAMMABLE SPRAY AND NEVER LEAVE IT UNATTENDED WHEN THE CANDLES ARE LIT.

1 Draw the shape for the lampshade on to a piece of chipboard: the base is 14.5 cm/ 5¾ in wide, the height 25 cm/10 in and the top 11 cm/4½ in wide. Using a metal ruler, craft knife and cutting mat, cut out the rectangle. You will need four identical pieces.

2 With a pencil and ruler, mark a line 8 mm/ ⅜ in from the edge along both long sides of each of the four pieces. Then mark a dot every 1 cm/½ in along each line.

3 Using the hole punch, make a hole on every pencil mark along each line. Rub out all the pencil marks.

4 Hold two of the sides together. Using a short length of string, tie a double knot through the topmost holes, cutting the ends very short. Repeat at every alternate hole. Ease each knot so that it sits flat against one side of the shade rather than leaving the knot on the corner edges. Repeat until all four pieces of chipboard are held together.

5 Assemble the simple table lamp. Place the lampshade over the lamp, guiding the flex gently between two of the sides so that it sits flat on a surface.

MATERIALS AND EQUIPMENT YOU WILL NEED

THICK UNLINED CHIPBOARD (YOU COULD USE THE BACK OF SKETCH BOOKS) • PENCIL • METAL RULER • CRAFT KNIFE • CUTTING MAT • REVOLVING HOLE PUNCH • RUBBER • STRING • SCISSORS • TWO-CORE FLEX • TWO-CORE FLEX SWITCH • PLUG • CANDLE LIGHTBULB • PENDANT LAMPHOLDER SUITABLE FOR TWO-CORE FLEX • 13 CM/5 IN WIRE LAMPSHADE HOLDER

# TASSELLED TIE-BACKS

THESE BEAUTIFUL TIE-BACKS MADE FROM CARDBOARD TASSELS AND SISAL ROPE WILL ADD A TOUCH OF OPULENCE TO YOUR DRAPES. MADE FROM BASIC CORRUGATED PACKING CARDBOARD, THE TASSELS ARE MADE TO LOOK LIKE TRADITIONAL CORD TASSELS AND THE THICK ROPE SPRAYED WITH GOLD PAINT SETS THEM OFF WELL. THE ROPE CAN BE BOUGHT FROM BOATING SHOPS AND IS A MUCH CHEAPER ALTERNATIVE TO THICK CORD. THE TIE-BACKS CAN BE LEFT UNPAINTED FOR A NATURAL LOOK OR SPRAYED WITH PAINT IN ANY COLOUR YOU LIKE. TRY SPRAYING THE TWO LAYERS OF STRIPS IN DIFFERENT COLOURS BEFORE GLUING THEM ON, TO GIVE A TWO-TONE EFFECT TO CO-ORDINATE WITH YOUR FABRICS AND FURNISHINGS.

1 Cut a piece of cardboard 35 cm x 14 cm/ 13¾ in x 5½ in. Cut an 80 cm/31½ in piece of rope. Wrap the cardboard around one end of the rope, smooth side out, lining up the edge with the end of the rope. Glue the end of the cardboard and secure in place.

2 Cut another piece of cardboard 25 cm x 6 cm/10 in x 2½ in. Again roll it around the rope, above the first piece, this time corrugated side out. Glue and secure in place.

3 Place a large piece of cardboard corrugated side down on your surface and using a pencil and ruler, draw lines 1.5 cm/⅝ in apart and 34 cm/13½ in long. Cut them out on a cutting mat using a metal ruler and craft knife. Repeat, but draw the lines 1 cm/½ in apart and 34 cm/13½ in long. You will need about ten of the wide strips and 16 of the narrow ones. ▶

## MATERIALS AND EQUIPMENT YOU WILL NEED

SINGLE-FACED CORRUGATED PACKING CARDBOARD • CRAFT KNIFE • CUTTING MAT • THICK SISAL ROPE • HIGH-TACK, FAST-DRYING GLUE • PENCIL • METAL RULER • GOLD SPRAY PAINT • PAPER FASTENER

4 Fold all the strips in half with the corrugated sides together. Dab some glue about 3 cm/1¼ in from the centre fold and hold in place until firmly stuck. Glue the wider strips around the main roll of cardboard.

5 Glue the narrower strips on top, slightly below the first row. Dab glue on to the back of the tops of the strips, press in place and hold until stuck firmly.

6 Measure and cut out a strip of cardboard 1.25 cm/⁹⁄₁₆ in wide and long enough to wrap around the tassel with a small overlap. Glue the flat side of the strip, wrap around the tassel and secure in place.

7 Cut a strip of cardboard 1.5 cm x 13 cm/⅝ in x 5 in long. Glue the corrugated side and wrap around the middle of the top roll. Cut another strip 4 mm/⅛ in wide and 24 cm/9½ in long. Dot glue along the first strip at regular intervals and stick the narrow strip on top, making loops between the dots of glue.

8 Cut a piece of cardboard 3 cm x 10 cm/ 1¼ in x 4 in. Wrap it around the rope above the tassel, glue the end and secure in place, ensuring that it is not stuck on to the rope (so that it can be moved up and down). Glue another strip measuring 8 mm x 10 cm/ ⅜ in x 4 in on the middle of the first one.

9 Make another tassel on the other end of the rope. Place the tassels and rope on some spare paper in a well-ventilated space and spray the whole thing with gold paint. Tilt the tassels up slightly so that the paint hits the underside of the strips and there is an even coverage. Leave to dry.

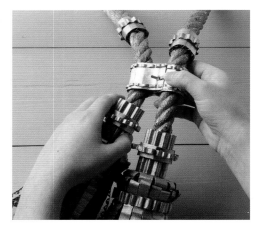

10 Cut a strip of cardboard 4 cm x 19 cm/1½ in x 7½ in. Stick narrow strips around both edges. Spray gold. Wrap the strip around both pieces of rope and push a paper fastener through all the layers. Turn over and pull apart the two prongs of the fastener so that they lie flat on the back of the cardboard.

# STORAGE BOXES

THESE LARGE STORAGE BOXES ARE IDEAL FOR STORING CLOTHES AND BEDDING. THEY CAN BE MADE TO ANY SIZE BY SIMPLY SCALING THE TEMPLATE UP OR DOWN, TO MAKE BOXES FOR SEWING ACCESSORIES, KITCHEN THINGS OR TO USE AS GIFT BOXES. MAKE SEVERAL BOXES AND LINE THEM UP WITH ALTERNATE CONCAVE AND CONVEX FRONTS TO CREATE A LOVELY WAVY EFFECT ALONG A SHELF. THE PAINTED MANILA PAPER AND ROPE KNOT HANDLE ADD TO THEIR UTILITARIAN LOOK BUT THE SHAPED ENDS ADD AN INTERESTING TWIST. TIE ON BROWN LUGGAGE LABELS WITH THE CONTENTS OF EACH BOX LISTED ON THEM FOR AN IDEAL STORAGE SOLUTION.

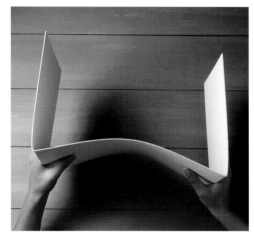

1 Using the diagrams in the back of the book as a guide, draw the six pieces of the box on to cardboard. Cut out one lid, one base, two side and two lid side pieces, using a craft knife and metal ruler for the straight edges.

2 On the side and lid side pieces, score along the short dotted lines as indicated, using a sharp instrument such as a bradawl. Fold the cardboard so that the score will be on the outside of the fold, to make the corners. Holding each side piece at the corners, bend it to curve and shape the cardboard, bending one side and one lid side piece to form a concave shape and the remaining side and lid side to form a convex shape (see Basic Techniques).

3 Dilute some cream paint to make a wash and paint lines freehand on to the manila paper using a piece of sponge cut into a 2.5 cm/1 in block. Leave the paint to dry thoroughly. ▶

## MATERIALS AND EQUIPMENT YOU WILL NEED

MEDIUM-WEIGHT BLEACHED CARDBOARD • PENCIL • CRAFT KNIFE • METAL RULER • CUTTING MAT • BRADAWL • CREAM WATER-BASED PAINT • MANILA PAPER • PIECE OF SPONGE • SCISSORS • WALLPAPER PASTE • GLUE • CLOTHES PEGS • CREAM ROPE

4 Cut the manila paper to the same size as the cardboard side pieces, allowing an extra 3 cm/1¼ in along the long edges. Stick the paper on to the cardboard using wallpaper paste. Fold and stick the border of manila paper along one edge of each of the four pieces. Snip into the other border at regular intervals with scissors.

6 Carefully tip the box on its side and glue the snipped edges all around the edges of the base. Leave it until completely dry.

8 Cut a piece of manila paper the same size as the lid template and glue in place on top of the box lid. Leave to dry.

5 Place the base flat and bend the side pieces around it, matching the centre markings. Glue the overlapping edges together and hold together with clothes pegs until completely dry and secure.

7 Place the lid flat and bend the lid side pieces around it, matching the centre markings. Glue the overlapping edges together and hold together with clothes pegs until completely dry and secure. Carefully tip the lid on its side and glue the snipped edges all around the edges of the lid in the same way as before.

9 Cut a hole in the centre of the lid, through the cardboard and paper layers. Make a knot near the end of the rope, thread the rope through the hole, then tie another knot, to make a knotted handle. Cut off any excess rope and fray the ends to make tassels.

# SHELF EDGING

EDGINGS ADD INTEREST TO PLAIN SHELVES AND CARDBOARD IS AN ECONOMICAL MATERIAL TO USE INSTEAD OF THE MORE TRADITIONAL LACE. CINNAMON STICKS GIVE OFF A LOVELY AROMA AS WELL AS BEING DECORATIVE AND WOULD FIT WELL ON A KITCHEN SHELF. FOR SHELVES IN A LINEN CUPBOARD, CHOOSE LITTLE BUNDLES OF LAVENDER INSTEAD. CARDBOARD EDGINGS LOOK GOOD ON FURNITURE TOO. TACK THEM ROUND THE TOP OF A TABLE OR GLUE THEM ALONG THE TOP OF CUPBOARD DOORS.

1 Draw a 12 cm/4¾ in equilateral triangle on a scrap of plain card. Cut out and use as a template. Place on the flat side of the grey fine flute corrugated cardboard and draw around it. Move the template along so that it slightly overlaps the right-hand corner of the drawn triangle. Draw around the template and continue along the cardboard.

2 Cut out the shelf edging. Draw a line 4 cm/1½ in from the top edge of each triangle, find the centre of each and put a pencil mark 7.5 mm/5⁄16 in on either side of this line. Punch holes along the shelf edging at each pencil mark.

3 Trace the template from the back of the book. Cut out a star shape from plain card. Punch holes where indicated. Draw around the template on to the back of a piece of black medium flute corrugated cardboard and mark the holes. Cut 2 cm/¾ in squares out of scraps of the corrugated cardboard, one for each triangle on your edging.

4 Make holes in the stars where marked. Punch holes in the small squares of cardboard about 1.5 cm/5⁄8 in apart.

5 Take a length of raffia and thread it through the shelf edging from the back to the front. Thread one of the small squares on to this. Put a small blob of glue on to each end of the raffia if it is split and difficult to thread through the holes.

6 Thread the raffia through the holes in one of the stars and tie with a knot on the front. On alternate triangles place a cinnamon stick across the raffia and secure with a tight knot. Push the upholstery tacks through the shelf edging where the triangles meet and gently tack to the edge of the shelf.

## MATERIALS AND EQUIPMENT YOU WILL NEED

PLAIN CARD FOR THE TEMPLATE • PENCIL • SCISSORS • GREY FINE FLUTE SINGLE-FACED CORRUGATED CARDBOARD • CRAFT KNIFE • CUTTING MAT • METAL RULER • REVOLVING HOLE PUNCH • TRACING PAPER • BLACK MEDIUM FLUTE SINGLE-FACED CORRUGATED CARDBOARD • DOUBLE WALL CORRUGATED CARDBOARD • RAFFIA • GLUE • CINNAMON STICKS • BRASS UPHOLSTERY TACKS • HAMMER

# PLACEMATS

THESE STYLISH PLACEMATS ARE VERY EASY TO MAKE AND ADD A CONTEMPORARY LOOK TO THE DINNER TABLE. THE SMALLER GENTLY CURVING FLOWER SHAPE COULD BE USED TO MAKE COASTERS, WITH NAPKINS TIED IN CO-ORDINATING COLOURED CORDS.

MOUNTING CARD IS AVAILABLE IN AN ARRAY OF BEAUTIFUL COLOURS, SO YOU CAN MATCH THE PLACEMATS TO YOUR CHINA. TO ADD EXTRA INTEREST, REVERSE THE COLOURS ON HALF OF THEM SO

THAT THEY CAN BE ARRANGED ALTERNATELY FOR A STRIKING LOOK. THE MATS CAN BE MADE IN ANY SIZE — MEASURE YOUR DINNER PLATES AND MAKE THE MATS LARGER SO THAT THEY WILL BE SEEN AROUND THE EDGE OF THE PLATE.

THE JOY OF CARDBOARD IS THAT IT IS VERY EASY TO WORK WITH AND EASILY RECYCLED, SO IF THE PLACEMATS GET DIRTY YOU CAN SIMPLY MAKE SOME MORE!

1 Using the diagram at the back of the book as a guide, make a template for the placemat. Draw around the template on to the mounting card.

3 Cut out both card shapes using a craft knife and a cutting mat. Ensure that the blade is very sharp and cut slowly and carefully so that the end result is very neat.

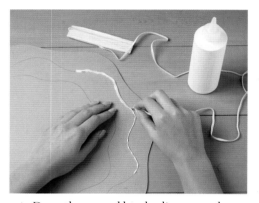

4 Draw the curved border line on to the base card in pencil. Apply a fine line of glue, following the drawn line, then carefully stick the flat cord over the glue line. Cut and butt up the cord ends where they meet.

2 Make a pattern piece in the same way for the smaller inside shape and draw it on to the other colour of card.

5 Glue the inside shape in place within the curved border.

MATERIALS AND EQUIPMENT YOU WILL NEED

TRACING PAPER • PENCIL • MEDIUM-WEIGHT MANILA CARD IN TWO COLOURS • CRAFT KNIFE • CUTTING MAT • HIGH-TACK GLUE • FLAT CORD

# STATIONERY FOLDER AND BOX

THIS STATIONERY FOLDER AND BOX CAN BE MADE TO FIT ANY SIZE OF PAPER AND ENVELOPES AND IS A GOOD PROJECT TO MAKE TO ORGANIZE YOUR WRITING DESK. TO GIVE IT A UTILITARIAN FEEL, THE CARDBOARD IS KEPT NATURAL AND THE PLAIN CANVAS IS FINISHED WITH ROUGH HAND STITCHING. IN KEEPING WITH THE STATIONERY THEME, THE FOLDER IS HELD TOGETHER WITH PAPER FASTENERS. THE FOLDER IS FINISHED WITH TWO LOOPS OF STITCHED CANVAS PINNED ON TO BOTH HALVES OF THE FRONT WITH A TWIGGY PENCIL ACTING AS A FASTENER.

THE CORRUGATED CARDBOARD USED INSIDE THE FOLDER IS AN EFFECTIVE PEN HOLDER BECAUSE PENCILS AND PENS FIT IN BETWEEN THE RIDGES IN THE CARDBOARD.

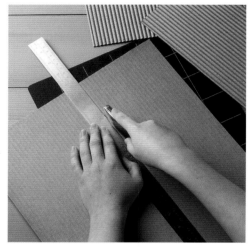

1 To make the folder, measure and cut out a rectangle of the single wall corrugated cardboard measuring 30 cm x 40 cm / 12 in x 16 in using the metal ruler, craft knife and cutting mat. Measure and cut out two pieces of the cardboard measuring 15 cm x 40 cm / 6 in x 16 in.

2 Take a sheet of the medium flute single-faced corrugated cardboard and measure three rectangles with the same dimensions as in step 1, drawing on to the flat side of the cardboard. Cut them out.

3 Measure two rectangles 40 cm x 10 cm / 16 in x 4 in on to the canvas. Cut out with sharp scissors.

## MATERIALS AND EQUIPMENT YOU WILL NEED

SINGLE WALL CORRUGATED CARDBOARD • PENCIL • METAL RULER • CRAFT KNIFE • CUTTING MAT • MEDIUM FLUTE SINGLE-FACED CORRUGATED CARDBOARD • NATURAL CANVAS • SCISSORS • DRESSMAKER'S PINS • EMBROIDERY THREAD IN CONTRASTING COLOUR • TAPESTRY NEEDLE • PAPER FASTENERS • TWIGGY PENCIL • HIGH-TACK GLUE • WOODEN SPOON

4 Turn over about 1 cm/½ in all the way round the canvas, folding the corners over first. Take a long length of embroidery thread, thread it through the needle and tie a knot in one end. Roughly stitch around the canvas from back to front. Do not worry about the stitches being too neat. Make sure that the needle goes through all the layers of fabric at the corners. Finish with a knot.

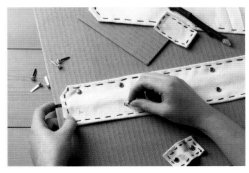

5 Make five pencil marks in the fabric at equal spaces and about 1 cm/½ in from both long edges. Make small slits with the scissors. Place the two smaller pieces of single wall cardboard at either side of the large rectangle and lay the canvas over the joins. Push the paper fasteners through the slits in the fabric and through the card, opening the clips out on the back. Continue until all the paper fasteners are in place on both pieces of canvas at either side of the large rectangle. Make two small strips of stitched canvas large enough to hold the twiggy pencil and attach them to the front of the folder, one on each front piece.

6 Cut a strip of canvas measuring 22 cm x 7.5 cm/8½ in x 3 in, then cut five right-angled triangles with two sides of 12 cm/4¾ in and a smaller strip long enough to hold your envelopes. Turn over all the edges and stitch with embroidery thread as before. Turn the corners of the triangles over first, as in step 4.

7 For the pen holder, cut slits in the long 22 cm/8½ in strip of canvas about 2 cm/¾ in apart. Check that your pens will slot through each loop. Position the canvas strip across the middle of one of the smaller pieces of medium flute single-faced corrugated cardboard. Fasten with paper fasteners. Cut slits in the corners of the triangles and fasten to the larger piece of medium flute cardboard, as shown.

8 Open out the folder and apply glue to the inside. Stick the three medium flute corrugated cardboard pieces on top of the single wall cardboard pieces and press down firmly to ensure adhesion. Put the pens, paper and envelopes into the folder. Close the folder and push the twiggy pencil through the two loops on the front to keep it closed. Pull the pencil out of one of the loops to open it.

9 To make the box, draw a rectangle on to another piece of the single wall corrugated cardboard 42 cm x 36 cm/16½ in x 14 in. Draw lines 10 cm/4 in from the edge on all four sides. Cut the whole rectangle out. Cut out two pieces measuring 8 cm x 22 cm/3¼ in x 8½ in for the lid flaps.

►

**10** Take the large rectangle, and draw flaps about 2 cm/¾ in wide on both ends of what will be the longest sides of the box. Draw a line cutting the corners off. Cut out the corner sections of the large rectangle on a cutting mat with the ruler and craft knife.

**12** Cut out two strips of canvas 22 cm x 5 cm/8½ in x 2 in and two strips measuring 22 cm x 7.5 cm/8½ in x 3 in. As before, fold over the edges by about 1 cm/ ½ in and stitch in place with embroidery thread. Cut four slits along both edges (about 1.25 cm/⁹⁄₁₆ in) on both of the shorter strips and attach the box and lid pieces with paper fasteners. Attach the longer strips on to the lid flaps. Tie them together to close the box.

**11** Use your thumb to score over the pencil lines along the length of the corrugated cardboard and use a wooden spoon against the direction of the ridges (see Basic Techniques). Bend the cardboard along the fold lines and make two small slits at each corner. Push a paper fastener through the slit and both pieces of cardboard to join the corners.

# SCREEN

THIS ELEGANT SCREEN IS BASED ON TRADITIONAL WOOD PANELLING. THE SIZE OF THE FINISHED SCREEN WILL PROBABLY DEPEND ON THE SIZE OF THE CARDBOARD YOU CAN FIND. TRY PACKAGING AND BOX-MAKING COMPANIES, WHICH WILL OFTEN SELL CARDBOARD CHEAPLY. IF LARGE PIECES ARE NOT AVAILABLE, YOU CAN MAKE THE PANELS OF THE SCREEN WITH SEPARATE PIECES, BUT MAKE SURE THAT THE JOINS ON EACH SIDE OF THE PANEL DO NOT FALL NEXT TO EACH OTHER AS THIS WILL WEAKEN THE SCREEN.

1 For each panel, cut two rectangles 120 cm x 60 cm/48 in x 24 in. Draw a line 12 cm/4¾ in from the edge all the way round one piece on the side that will not show. Draw a line across the middle of the panel and measure 6 cm/2½ in above and below this line so that there is a 12 cm/4¾ in strip across the cardboard. Cut out the two inside rectangles.

2 On scrap paper, draw a rectangle 44 cm x 28 cm/17½ in x 11 in. Draw another one 2 cm/¾ in inside this one. Mark the centre horizontally and vertically. Using a paint can or plate, draw curves at each corner, one at each end and two curves along the longest edges, using the centre lines as a guide.

3 Cut out the paper shape and tape it on to the wrong side of one of the cardboard rectangles. Draw around it and cut it out. You will need two of these shapes for each screen panel. Measure and cut out two rectangles 17 cm x 33 cm/6¾ in x 13 in for each panel.

4 Spread glue all over the wrong side of one of the front screen panels and fit it on to the back. Apply glue to the back of the curved shape and stick it in the middle of each panel. Finally, glue the rectangle of cardboard in the centre. Repeat for each panel.

5 Turn the panel over. Mark 10 cm/4 in from the bottom of the screen and 2.5 cm/1 in from the long edge. Mark 10 cm/4 in from that and 10 cm/4 in from that. Repeat at the top of the panel and in the middle. Punch holes where marked.

6 Place two panels next to each other, lining up the holes. Cut a 60 cm/24 in length of string and wrap tape round the ends. Thread through the first two holes from the front to the back. Take one of the ends, cross it over and lace it through the next diagonal hole. Repeat for the other end. Lift the screen up slightly, cross the two ends over and thread through the diagonal holes again. Knot the ends together. Repeat with the other holes. Join all three panels.

MATERIALS AND EQUIPMENT YOU WILL NEED

Brown fine flute single wall corrugated cardboard • Metal ruler • Pencil • Craft knife • Cutting mat • Scrap paper • Paint can or small plate • Scissors • Masking tape • Rubber solution glue • Revolving hole punch • String

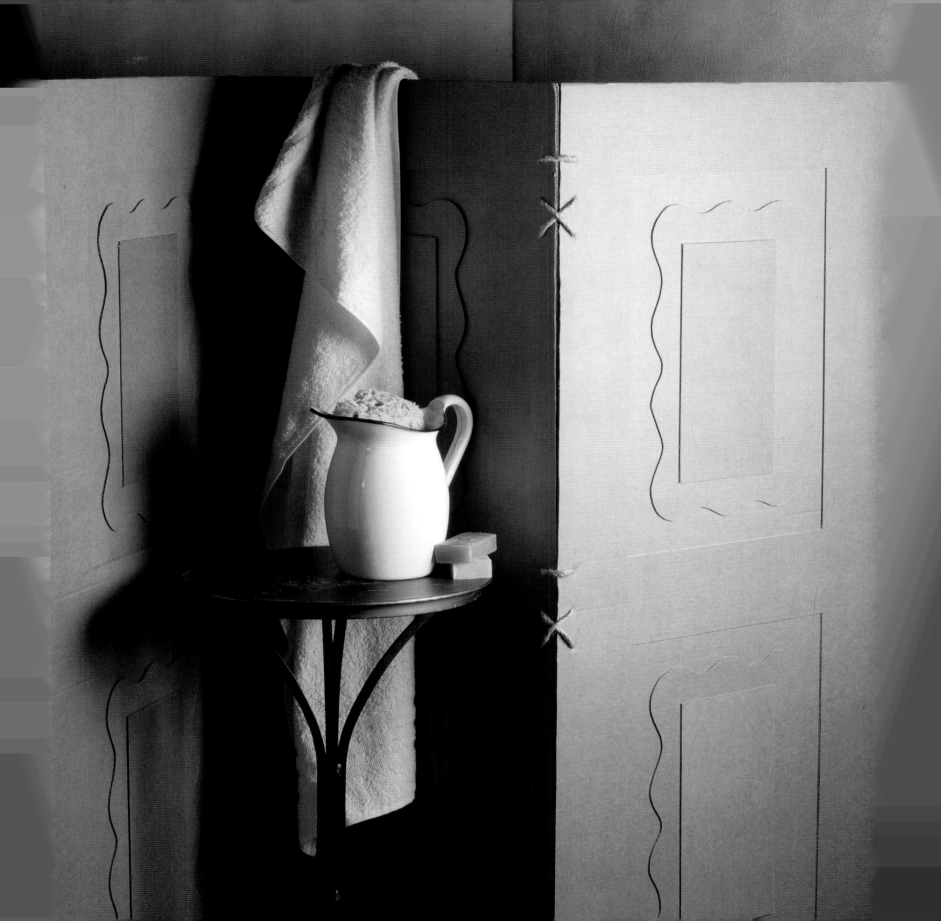

# WASTE PAPER BIN

THIS SIMPLE WASTE PAPER BIN HAS A VERY CONTEMPORARY SHAPE WITH ITS SLIGHTLY CURVED RIM AND METAL STUDS. THE LARGE EYELET MAKES A USEFUL HANDLE. THE FLECKED CARDBOARD IS MADE FROM RECYCLED NEWSPAPER, WHICH CARRIES THROUGH THE THEME OF WASTE PAPER, GIVING A WITTY CROSS REFERENCE. TO ADD THE EYELET AS DECORATION ON THE WASTE PAPER BIN, YOU WILL NEED A LARGE EYELET PUNCH. THESE ARE AVAILABLE FROM BOATING AND LEATHER GOODS SUPPLIERS.

1 Using the diagram at the back of the book as a guide, draw the shape on to the recycled cardboard. If this is very thin, stick two layers together. Cut out the shape. Decide where the eyelet should go and draw around the inside. Cut out this circle, being careful not to go over the pencil line.

2 Place the bottom of the eyelet punch on a solid surface and lay the larger section of the eyelet on top. Put the cardboard over this with the eyelet through the hole. Place the ring of the eyelet around the hole, then put the punch on top and hammer several times.

3 On the inside of one straight edge of the bin, draw a line 1 cm/½ in from the edge. Do the same on the outside of the other edge. Put pencil marks every 5 cm/2 in apart down both lines. Make holes at every mark large enough for the metal studs to fit through snugly. Glue the two edges together so that the pencil lines do not show and the holes match up.

4 Push one half of a metal stud through one of the holes, insert the other half from the other side of the bin and hammer in place on a solid surface. Continue along the line of holes until all the studs are securely in place.

5 Draw a circle on another piece of recycled cardboard with a radius of 10.5 cm/4¼ in. Draw another circle inside this with a radius of 9 cm/3½ in, using the same centre. Cut out the larger circle. Score a line along the inner circle with a craft knife, being careful not to cut into the cardboard.

6 Cut triangles from the outside edge of the circle to the inner circle about 1.5 cm/⅝ in apart. Do not cut into the inner circle. Continue all the way round. Fold the flaps down and apply glue to the outside of the flaps. Push the circle into the bin until it is level and sits comfortably inside. Leave to dry.

MATERIALS AND EQUIPMENT YOU WILL NEED

TRACING PAPER • PENCIL • RECYCLED NEWSPAPER CARDBOARD • SPRAY ADHESIVE • CRAFT KNIFE • CUTTING MAT • METAL RULER •
35 MM/1½ IN DIAMETER METAL EYELET • LARGE EYELET PUNCH • HAMMER • REVOLVING HOLE PUNCH • METAL STUDS • GLUE • PAIR OF COMPASSES • SCISSORS

# LAMPBASE

THIS SIMPLE AND ELEGANT LAMPBASE IS MADE FROM CORRU-
GATED PACKING CARDBOARD CUT INTO DIFFERENT-SIZED STRIPS
AND GLUED AROUND A CENTRAL CORE. BUY THE LIGHT FITTINGS
FROM AN ELECTRICAL SHOP AND SIMPLY THREAD THE FLEX THROUGH
THE HOLE RUNNING DOWN THE CENTRE OF THE LAMPBASE. IF THE
LAMPBASE IS UNSTEADY, YOU CAN STICK IT ON TO A CIRCLE OF WOOD
TO MAKE IT SECURE. IF THE CARDBOARD FLUTES BECOME SQUASHED
DURING ROLLING, CAREFULLY RE-FORM THEM WITH YOUR FINGERS.

1 Make the base by cutting a rectangle of corrugated cardboard measuring 120 cm x 40 cm/47 in x 15¾ in. Apply glue over the smooth side of the cardboard and roll it up, leaving a central hole to insert the flex. Try to keep the roll tight to make the lampbase more stable. Hold the cardboard in place until the glue is dry.

2 Cut more strips of corrugated cardboard, varying the sizes, and glue these around the main roll. Use a long length to glue around the bottom to create a solid base. Hold the glued cardboard in place until it is stuck firmly.

3 Cut narrower strips of cardboard and glue these around the larger ones. Try them in different positions before gluing, until you are happy with the arrangement.

4 Thread the flex with the lampholder attached through the central hole until the lampholder sits on the top of the lampbase.

5 Using a craft knife, carefully cut a groove from the centre to the edge of the base of the lampbase large enough for the flex to sit comfortably in. Lay the flex in the groove and tape in place. Alternatively, stick a circle of fabric or thin cardboard on the base.

MATERIALS AND EQUIPMENT YOU WILL NEED

SINGLE-FACED CORRUGATED PACKING CARDBOARD • METAL RULER • CRAFT KNIFE • CUTTING MAT • HIGH-TACK, FAST-DRYING GLUE •
THREE-CORE GOLD FLEX • LAMPHOLDER WITH 7.5 CM/3 IN THREADED ROD AND BRASS SWITCH • MASKING TAPE •
PLUG • LIGHT-BULB

# DOLL'S HOUSE

THIS QUIRKY DOLL'S HOUSE IS MADE BY SLOTTING TOGETHER THICK GREY CHIPBOARD. ITS ANGLES AND ASYMMETRY GIVE IT A RATHER RAMSHACKLE LOOK, AND THE CARDBOARD PILLARS AND SCROLLS REMOVE IT FROM THE TRADITIONAL DOLL'S HOUSE DESIGN. THE HOUSE COULD BE PAINTED WITH WATER-BASED PAINTS AND DECORATED INSIDE WITH WRAPPING PAPER OR SCRAPS OF FABRIC. ENCOURAGE CHILDREN TO MAKE THEIR OWN CARDBOARD FURNITURE FOR THEIR TOYS. THE TWO FRONT PIECES COULD BE MADE SLIGHTLY LONGER AND LEFT WITHOUT HINGES SO THAT THEY CAN JUST BE PROPPED UP AGAINST THE HOUSE AND REMOVED COMPLETELY FOR PLAYING.

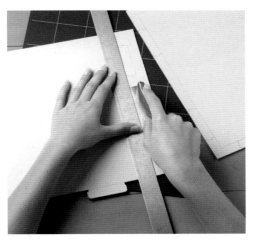

1 Using the diagrams from the back of the book as a guide, make templates for the front and the back of the doll's house. Transfer on to the chipboard. Mark the position of the window on the front piece and cut out, then cut the piece in half. Mark the positions of the slits in the back piece and carefully cut them out using a sharp craft knife, cutting mat and metal ruler.

2 Draw the two side pieces for the house on to chipboard. Cut them out, cutting carefully round the tabs. Cut out the windows and the slits where marked.

3 Draw the two floor pieces on to the chipboard and carefully cut them out. You may need to change the blade frequently to ensure that the craft knife is always sharp. ▶

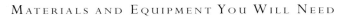

## MATERIALS AND EQUIPMENT YOU WILL NEED

TRACING PAPER • PENCIL • THICK UNLINED GREY CHIPBOARD • CRAFT KNIFE • CUTTING MAT • METAL RULER • HIGH-TACK GLUE • SINGLE-FACED CORRUGATED PACKING CARDBOARD • SCISSORS • STRONG GLUE • GLUE GUN (OPTIONAL) • METAL HINGES

4 Score along the flap at the front of the floor piece and gently fold it over. Lay the back piece on the surface and slot the two floor pieces into this. Slot the side pieces into the back and floor pieces, easing them in gently by carefully bending the chipboard.

5 For the roof, cut out a 64 cm x 32 cm/ 25½ in x 13 in rectangle from the chipboard. Mark a line down the middle of the length. Score along the line lightly. Cut two extra pieces measuring 29 cm x 28 cm/ 11½ in x 11 in.

6 Glue the two pieces of chipboard on to each half of the roof piece a few millimetres from the central score line. Carefully bend the roof so that it folds along the score line. Apply glue along the top of the two side walls and the back of the house, then stick the roof in place, butting up the panels inside the roof to the glued edges. For extra strength, glue a triangle of cardboard inside the roof.

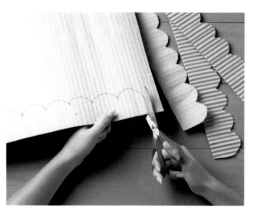

7 Using the diagram in the back of the book as a guide, draw the tile pieces on to the back of the corrugated cardboard. Cut out with scissors. Starting from the bottom, glue the tiles on to the roof, overlapping them slightly, until the whole roof is covered. Cut a strip of cardboard along the corrugated ridges and glue to the ridge of the roof.

8 Cut out rectangles of corrugated cardboard for the pillars, 6 cm x 32 cm/ 2½ in x 13 in and 6 cm x 30 cm/2½ in x 12 in. Bend them over slightly and glue them on to each front piece. Make scrolls out of strips of cardboard, securing them with glue. Cut out the awnings using the templates at the back of the book and stick along the roof edge of the fronts. Cut strips of corrugated cardboard to edge the windows and door, and glue in position.

9 Hold each front piece against the house in the required position and make two marks inside on the front panel and side wall for the hinges. Glue the hinges in place, using strong glue and a glue gun if necessary. Glue a strip of corrugated cardboard along the edges of the front of the roof. Cut out curtain shapes and brick shapes and glue in place.

# TRUG

THIS UNUSUAL TRUG IS A GOOD WAY OF RECYCLING OLD FRUIT BOXES. TRY TO FIND LARGE FRUIT BOXES — APPLE BOXES ARE IDEAL. SMALL FRUIT AND VEGETABLE BOXES TEND TO BE MADE FROM VERY THICK CARDBOARD WHICH WILL NOT BEND. SAVE THE LONGEST LENGTHS OF CARDBOARD FOR THE FINAL STRIPS ACROSS THE BOTTOM

OF THE BASKET. A HEAVY-DUTY STAPLER IS NEEDED TO STAPLE THE SEVERAL LAYERS OF CARDBOARD TOGETHER.

THE BASKET CAN BE USED AS A TRADITIONAL GARDEN TRUG FOR CARRYING CUT FLOWERS AND TOOLS OR IT COULD BE MADE WITH-OUT THE HANDLE AND USED AS A FRUIT BOWL.

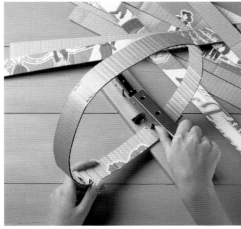  

1 Cut long strips from the fruit boxes 4 cm/1½ in wide using a metal ruler, craft knife and cutting mat. Take two of the strips and join them together by overlapping the ends slightly and stapling them in place.

2 The strips of cardboard need to be bent slightly to make the trug. To do this, hold a strip with your left hand, gripping it between your thumb and the edge of your forefinger. Take the end of the strip with your right hand and pull it through your left hand, curving the cardboard. Repeat with all the cardboard strips.

3 Peg a strip across the loop of cardboard. Take a joined strip of cardboard and peg in position across the loop, bisecting the first strip at right angles. Staple together.

▶

## MATERIALS AND EQUIPMENT YOU WILL NEED
SINGLE WALL CARDBOARD FRUIT BOXES • METAL RULER • CRAFT KNIFE • CUTTING MAT •
HEAVY-DUTY STAPLER AND STAPLES • CLOTHES PEGS • PAINTBRUSH • MATT POLYURETHANE VARNISH

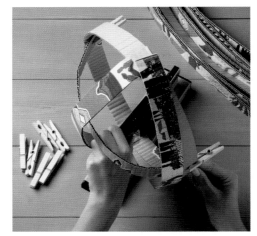

4 Staple a strip from one end of the loop to the other, overlapping each end over the strip already stapled on to it. Run it along the bottom of the loop. Always peg the strips in position to check that they are in the right place before stapling them. Cut off any excess cardboard at the end.

5 Continue to peg and then staple the strips across the initial loop, overlapping the edges slightly. Staple strips on alternate sides of the loop and keep checking that they are even on each side, otherwise they will not meet properly in the middle. Use the first stapled strip and the pegged strip as guides.

6 Keeping the longest strips for the bottom, peg and staple the last strip in place, overlapping the last strip on either side of the basket. Press the stapler firmly, as the staples will need to go through several layers of cardboard.

7 Take two strips and curve one of them the other way so that the plain side curves upwards. Hold these together and peg on to the basket to make a handle. When they are in the right position, staple them firmly in place, using several staples on each side.

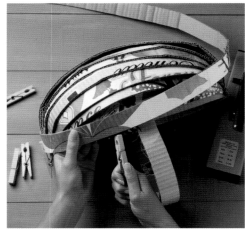

8 Join two more of the strips by stapling them together as before. This will be the rim of the basket. Peg it in place all the way round the top of the basket and staple in position approximately every 10 cm/4 in, ensuring that the staples go through all of the layers.

9 When all the strips are in place, rest the basket on some scrap paper and paint with varnish. Paint along the strips and dab the varnish outside and inside the basket. Apply extra layers of varnish if you need a tougher finish, but ensure that each layer of varnish is completely dry before applying another. The varnish may discolour the cardboard slightly, so test it out on a spare piece first.

# PELMET

PELMETS ARE PRACTICAL AS WELL AS DECORATIVE IN THAT THEY DISGUISE CURTAIN HEADINGS AND POLES AND ARE AN EFFECTIVE WAY OF FINISHING WINDOW TREATMENTS.

THIS CARDBOARD PELMET USES WOOD AS ITS BASE TO MAKE IT MORE DURABLE. THE FINE FLUTE CORRUGATED CARDBOARD HAS BEEN DECORATED WITH STARS, BEADING AND FRINGING MADE OF CORRUGATED PACKING CARDBOARD. RAFFIA TASSELS COMPLETE THE EFFECT. THE PELMET CAN BE MADE TO FIT ANY SIZE OF WINDOW, HOWEVER BEAR IN MIND THAT IT SHOULD NOT DOMINATE THE WINDOW BUT ADD THE FINISHING TOUCH AND FIT IN WITH THE OVER-ALL SCHEME OF THE ROOM. IT CAN BE USED WITHOUT CURTAINS AS A PURELY DECORATIVE FEATURE, AS HERE.

1 Cut two pieces of wood 15 cm/6 in long and one piece 90 cm/36 in long. Sand all the edges smooth.

2 Apply wood glue to one end of each of the short pieces and hold them at right angles at either end of the longer piece. Hold in position until the glue has partially dried. Tack in place using the tacks and hammer.

3 Cut a piece of plywood 17.5 cm x 90 cm/7 in x 36 in for the top of the pelmet. Spread glue along one edge of the pelmet frame and position the plywood on top. Tack in position. Wipe away any excess glue with a soft cloth. ▶

## MATERIALS AND EQUIPMENT YOU WILL NEED

1.2 M/48 IN OF 2.5 CM X 10 CM/1 IN X 4 IN WOOD • SAW • TAPE MEASURE • SANDPAPER • WOOD GLUE • TACKS • HAMMER • PLYWOOD • SOFT CLOTH • TRACING PAPER • PENCIL • GREY FINE FLUTE SINGLE-FACED CORRUGATED CARDBOARD • MASKING TAPE • METAL RULER • CRAFT KNIFE • CUTTING MAT • LARGE FLUTE SINGLE-FACED CORRUGATED PACKING CARDBOARD • SMALL SCISSORS • RAFFIA • HIGH-TACK GLUE • DRESSMAKER'S PINS • L-SHAPED BRACKETS • SCREWDRIVER • SCREWS

4 Using the diagram at the back of the book, make a template for the pelmet. Place the fine corrugated cardboard on the work surface smooth side up. You may need to join two pieces together – butt them up exactly and run a piece of tape along the edges to be joined. Draw a rectangle 34 cm x 110 cm/13½ in x 43¼ in. Draw a line 10 cm/4 in from each side edge. Draw a horizontal line 25 cm/10 in from the bottom of the cardboard. Place the template along the top edge of the large rectangle and draw the shaped edge.

6 Cut a long strip of corrugated packing cardboard about 6 cm/2½ in wide. Make rough snips all the way along the strip a few millimetres apart. Do not worry if some of the strips come off. Cut enough to edge the whole pelmet.

8 Enlarge the template of the star to size. Cut out three stars measuring 12 cm/ 4¾ in from the corrugated packing cardboard. Mark the centre of each star, then score lines from the centre to each point. Turn over and score from the centre to the nearest points on the corrugated side. Gently fold along the score lines to make them three-dimensional.

5 Cut out the shaped piece and cut away the two 10 cm/4 in corner pieces. Using a craft knife and metal ruler, gently score along the pencil lines, making sure that you do not cut into the cardboard. Carefully fold the cardboard over. Apply glue over the wooden frame and glue the cardboard in place.

7 Cut two pieces of spare cardboard about 12 cm/4¾ in square. Hold the end of a handful of raffia at the bottom and bind it around both pieces about four times, ending at the same place where you started. Thread a couple of strands of raffia through the two pieces of cardboard and pull up to the top. Tie with a secure knot. Slip the blade of a pair of scissors between the two pieces of cardboard and cut the tassel off. Wrap a few strands of raffia around the tassel about 3 cm/1¼ in from the top. Make another tassel in the same way.

9 From the grey cardboard cut a diamond slightly larger than the big star and stick it in the middle of the pelmet with the corrugated lines horizontal. Edge with strips of packing cardboard cut along the corrugated ridges and glued in position. Glue the stars on either side, then glue the fringed edging in place, pinning it until it has dried. Tape the tassels in place. Secure the pelmet to the wall with the L-shaped brackets.

# OAK LEAF FRAME

THIS ORNATE BAROQUE "GILT" PICTURE FRAME, DECORATED WITH OAK LEAVES, IS BASED ON A TRADITIONAL FRAME. FOLDING THE LEAVES SLIGHTLY AND ARRANGING THEM IRREGULARLY GIVES THE FRAME MORE DEPTH.

THIS PROJECT HIGHLIGHTS THE VERSATILITY OF CARDBOARD, TURNING IT FROM A PLAIN, BASIC MATERIAL INTO SOMETHING MUCH MORE ORNATE WHICH, WHEN SPRAYED GOLD, CAN EVEN EMULATE TRADITIONAL GILDING.

1 Cut a rectangle measuring 40 cm x 48 cm/16 in x 19 in from the medium flute corrugated cardboard. Draw a smaller rectangle inside this 14 cm/5½ in from the edge. Cut out the centre opening on a cutting mat.

2 On the smooth side of the fine flute corrugated cardboard, draw a line 2 cm/¾ in from the edge and then parallel lines 3 cm/1¼ in, 2 cm/¾ in, 6 cm/2½ in, 1.5 cm/⅝ in, 1.5 cm/⅝ in and 5 mm/¼ in apart from each other. Cut along this last line (strip measures 16.5 cm/6¾ in wide). Cut two lengths 48 cm/19 in long.

3 Cut the corners off the 2 cm/¾ in strip. Using a craft knife and metal ruler, gently score along the parallel lines, being careful not to cut the cardboard. Cut the opposite corners at a 45-degree angle, from the end of the second line to the edge of the cardboard.

4 Fold the cardboard along the score lines. Draw a line along each side of the frame 12 cm/4¾ in from the edge. Glue the strip with the corners cut off along the edge of the long side of the frame. Fold the cardboard over, lining up the edge with the pencil line, and glue in place. ▶

## MATERIALS AND EQUIPMENT YOU WILL NEED

MEDIUM FLUTE SINGLE WALL CORRUGATED CARDBOARD • METAL RULER • PENCIL • CRAFT KNIFE • CUTTING MAT •
FINE FLUTE SINGLE-FACED CORRUGATED CARDBOARD • HIGH-TACK GLUE • LARGE FLUTE SINGLE-FACED CORRUGATED PACKING CARDBOARD • CARD FOR TEMPLATES •
TRACING PAPER • SCISSORS • GOLD SPRAY PAINT

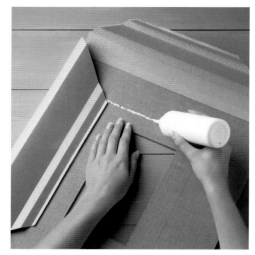

5 Cut two more strips of the scored cardboard 40 cm / 16 in long for the top and bottom of the frame. Cut off the corners and stick these two strips and the remaining long piece in place. It does not matter if the corners do not meet exactly. Leave to dry.

6 Cut a strip of large flute corrugated packing cardboard 2 cm / ¾ in wide and stick it along the inner strip of the frame as shown. Mitre the corners.

7 Trace the leaf-shaped template from the back of the book and enlarge to size. Cut out small and large oak leaf shapes from the fine flute and large flute cardboard. Score a line along each leaf on the smooth or corrugated side so that they can be bent a little.

8 Trace the second template from the back of the book and enlarge to size. Cut out four shapes from large flute cardboard. Fold them over, smooth side out, and glue the ends together. Cut strips of cardboard about 1 cm / ½ in wide and 50 cm / 20 in long. Loop them over three times and glue together at the bottom. Glue on to the first shape. Repeat on the other three and glue one to the middle of each side of the frame.

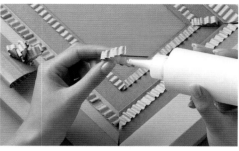

9 Cut strips of large flute cardboard about 1 cm / ½ in wide and edge the frame opening, leaving a gap a few millimetres from the edge. Glue a small loop of cardboard to each corner.

10 Make four more loops of large flute cardboard strips and secure with glue. Stick one to each corner. Arrange the leaves in the desired design, overlapping them slightly. When you are happy with the design, glue them all in place.

11 When the glue is dry, put the frame on some scrap paper in a well-ventilated space and spray with gold paint. Spray the underside of the leaves, covering them as evenly as you can with the paint.

# CLOCK

THIS SUNBURST CLOCK WITH ITS GENTLE RADIATING CURVES IS MADE BY GENTLY SCORING AND FOLDING THIN CHIPBOARD. A SIMPLE BATTERY-OPERATED CLOCK MECHANISM CAN BE BOUGHT FROM CRAFT SUPPLIERS AND IS EASY TO SLOT THROUGH THE CHIP-BOARD CLOCK FACE, OR OLD CLOCK PARTS WITH ORNATE HANDS CAN BE USED INSTEAD. GILT CREAM GIVES A MATT GOLD FINISH THAT IS DIFFERENT FROM THE FINISH OF METALLIC PAINT. APPLYING THIS OVER DEEP RED PAINT GIVES THE GOLD A DEEPER, ANTIQUE LOOK.

1 Trace the templates from the back of the book and enlarge to your required size. Draw the main clock shape on to the chipboard. Cut out the inner shape and the two hands with a craft knife and metal ruler. Do the same on the main clock shape, but cut the curved part out freehand with the craft knife.

2 Score along all the pencil lines gently on the front of the clock face with the craft knife, being careful not to cut the chipboard. Do the same on the inner piece. Score along the lines on the hands.

3 Turn the chipboard over, draw lines on the back, and score, as before. Turn the inner piece over and score along the lines on that as well.

4 Gently fold along all the score lines ensuring that the chipboard does not crease. Concertina the fold lines together to make the folds. Do the same with the centre piece. Paint all the pieces with the red paint and leave to dry.

5 Using a soft cloth, gently wipe the gilt cream all over the clock slightly unevenly so that some of the red paint just shows through. Leave to dry.

6 Cut holes into the middle of the back and front pieces of the clock and push through the clock mechanism. Screw on the metal screw. Glue the cardboard hands on to the plastic ones and push on to the clock.

MATERIALS AND EQUIPMENT YOU WILL NEED

TRACING PAPER • PENCIL • PAPER FOR TEMPLATE • THIN UNLINED CHIPBOARD • CRAFT KNIFE • METAL RULER • CUTTING MAT •
DEEP RED WATER-BASED PAINT • PAINTBRUSH • SOFT CLOTH • GILT CREAM • CLOCK PARTS

# CHANDELIER

THIS ELEGANT CHANDELIER WILL LIGHT UP ANY DINNER PARTY. MADE IN THE STYLE OF A TRADITIONAL CRYSTAL CHANDELIER, WITH STRINGS OF BEADS AND CRYSTAL-SHAPED DROPLETS, IT IS AN EXTREMELY CHEAP ALTERNATIVE. USING A CARDBOARD TUBE AS ITS CENTRAL CORE, THE ARMS ARE MADE FROM GALVANIZED WIRE, THEN COVERED IN CORRUGATED PACKING CARDBOARD. SMALL METAL PÂTISSERIE TINS ARE USED AS THE CANDLE HOLDERS FOR CANDLES OR NIGHTLIGHTS. MAKE SURE THAT THESE ARE NOT TOO HEAVY OR THE ARMS WILL DIP TOO MUCH AND THE CHANDELIER WILL LOSE ITS DELICATE SHAPE. NEVER LEAVE THE LIGHTED CANDLES UNATTENDED.

1 Measure a 28 cm/11 in length of thick cardboard tube and cut with a saw. You may need to sand the cut edge.

2 Draw a line round the tube 3 cm/1¼ in from the end. Mark six pencil marks on the line, measuring them with a tape measure to ensure that they are about the same distance apart. Using the bradawl, make holes at these points. Make three holes about 2 cm/¾ in from the other end, with equal spaces between them.

3 Cut six lengths of wire 110 cm/44 in long using wire cutters. Take one piece of wire and hold it against the bottom of the glass candle holder. Carefully bend the wire so that it coils around the candle holder two to three times. Then bend the wire down into a curve. Use the first coil of wire as a guide for the remaining five wires, so that they are all the same shape.

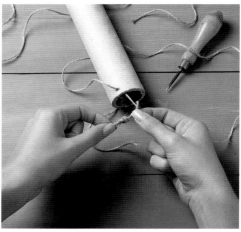

4 Cut three lengths of string measuring 60 cm/24 in long. Thread them through the holes at the top of the tube, securing them with a large knot inside the tube. Put tape on the end of the string if it will not go through the holes easily. Tie the three pieces of string together near the ends with a knot. ▶

## MATERIALS AND EQUIPMENT YOU WILL NEED

TAPE MEASURE • PENCIL • THICK CARDBOARD TUBE • SAW • FINE SANDPAPER • BRADAWL • 2 MM/0.078 IN GALVANIZED WIRE • WIRE CUTTERS • GLASS CANDLE HOLDER • STRING • MASKING TAPE • LARGE FLUTE SINGLE-FACED CORRUGATED PACKING CARDBOARD • HIGH-TACK GLUE • TRACING PAPER • MEDIUM FLUTE SINGLE-FACED CORRUGATED CARDBOARD • CRAFT KNIFE • CUTTING MAT • SCISSORS • METAL RULER • SIX PÂTISSERIE TINS

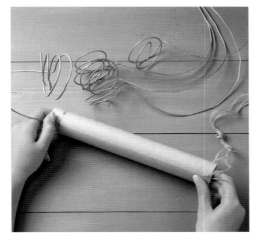

5 Push the straight end of one of the wire arms through a hole in the bottom of the tube and feed it through to the top. Bend the end of the wire over the top of the tube – about 2 cm/¾ in. Do the same with the five remaining wire arms.

7 Cut strips of large flute corrugated packing cardboard 2.5 cm/1 in wide and long enough to cover the coils of wire. Apply glue to the flat side. Glue around the coiled ends of the wire arm, and hold in place until stuck firmly.

9 Trace the bead templates from the back of the book. Draw about 150 small shapes (75 round ones, 75 elongated ones) and six droplet shapes on the medium flute corrugated cardboard. Cut out with a craft knife on a cutting mat.

6 Cut lengths of large flute corrugated packing cardboard 1.5 cm/⅝ in wide and long enough to run down the tube and along the arm of the chandelier, plus about 10 cm/ 4 in extra. Coil the end of the strip over at the end and glue the strip down the tube and along the wire arm. Glue another strip along the underside of the arm. Hold in place until the glue has dried. Do the same on the remaining five arms.

8 Roll up strips of large flute packing cardboard tightly and then let go to make loose coils. Make 12 coils and stick six on the bottom of the tube between the long strips and six on the underside of the arms.

10 Cut 12 lengths of string and thread the cardboard beads on to them – 12 on each string. You will need 12 strings of beads. Glue on to the chandelier from the top of the tube to the arms, draping them slightly. Thread string through the droplets, add a bead, then tie and glue them on to the underside of the coils of wire at the ends of the arms. Finish by gluing strips of card around the top and bottom of the tube. Hang the chandelier up with the string at the top of the tube, which can be altered to any length. Place pâtisserie tins in the wire coils.

# TRAY

GLUING TOGETHER LAYERS OF SINGLE WALL CORRUGATED CARD-BOARD MAKES A STURDY TRAY, ALTHOUGH ONE THAT IS MORE FOR DECORATION THAN EVERYDAY USE. THE HANDLES, MADE BY PUSHING PAPER FASTENERS THROUGH THE CARDBOARD AND THEN BENDING THEM INSIDE THE ROLLED HANDLE, ARE SURPRISINGLY STRONG. USE CARDBOARD THAT HAS A VERY FLAT, SMOOTH LAYER ON AT LEAST ONE SIDE, RATHER THAN CARDBOARD THAT SHOWS FLUTE LINES, FOR A SMARTER LOOK. THE TRAY COULD BE VARNISHED TO MAKE IT MORE ROBUST OR IT COULD BE PAINTED OR DECORATED WITH COLLAGE OR DECOUPAGE AND THEN VARNISHED.

1 On the cardboard draw out ten rectangles 38 cm x 50 cm / 15 in x 20 in. Cut them out on the cutting mat using the metal ruler and craft knife. Draw the pencil lines on the wrong side of the cardboard (not the side that will show).

2 Draw a line 5 cm / 2 in from the edge on six pieces of the cardboard, and cut out the centre rectangle on each one. Put the spare pieces aside to use for the handles.

3 Take one of the large pieces of cardboard and again measure 5 cm / 2 in from the edge all the way round. Draw an equilateral triangle measuring 3 cm / 1¼ in on a piece of spare card. Cut it out. Starting at the centre and working towards the corners, place the triangle template along the inner side of one of the pencil lines and draw around it, again on the wrong side of the cardboard.

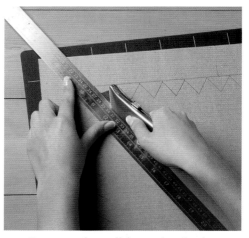

4 Continue along all four sides, finishing with a square at each corner. Cut out around the triangles, cutting from the pencil line to the point of the triangles. ▶

MATERIALS AND EQUIPMENT YOU WILL NEED
SINGLE WALL CORRUGATED CARDBOARD • PENCIL • METAL RULER • CRAFT KNIFE • CUTTING MAT •
TRACING PAPER • TWO LARGE METAL PAPER FASTENERS • HIGH-TACK GLUE

5 On two of the remaining complete pieces of cardboard, draw lines 7.5 cm/3 in from the edges all the way round. Cut out the inner rectangles and discard.

7 Following the diagram in the back of the book, make a template for the handle. Cut out a cardboard triangle and cut holes as indicated. Peel off one side of the cardboard.

9 Push the roll down on to the cardboard stems. Spread glue on the underside of the loose flap of cardboard and press in place. Hold firmly until the glue is dry.

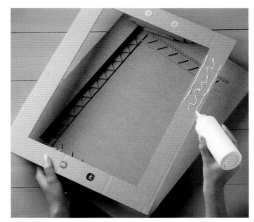

6 On the back of one of the first pieces of cardboard, measure two points 10 cm/ 4 in apart on either side of the centre of each short side. Make small slits with a craft knife. Insert a paper fastener into each slit from the wrong side. Cut pieces of cardboard measuring 3 cm x 5 cm/1¼ in x 2 in and peel the back off (see Basic Techniques). Wrap them round the base of the paper fasteners and glue in position.

8 Roll up the triangle of cardboard quite tightly and hold it firmly in position. Push the roll on to the paper fasteners. It should slot on to the fasteners quite easily. If it does not, then push firmly so that the fasteners push through the cardboard.

10 Lay the remaining complete piece of cardboard right side up on your work surface. Glue the back of each piece. Glue on the two pieces with rectangles cut out, then the piece with the triangular edge. Finally glue the six rectangular frames on top of each other, finishing with the handles. Wipe away any excess glue with your finger.

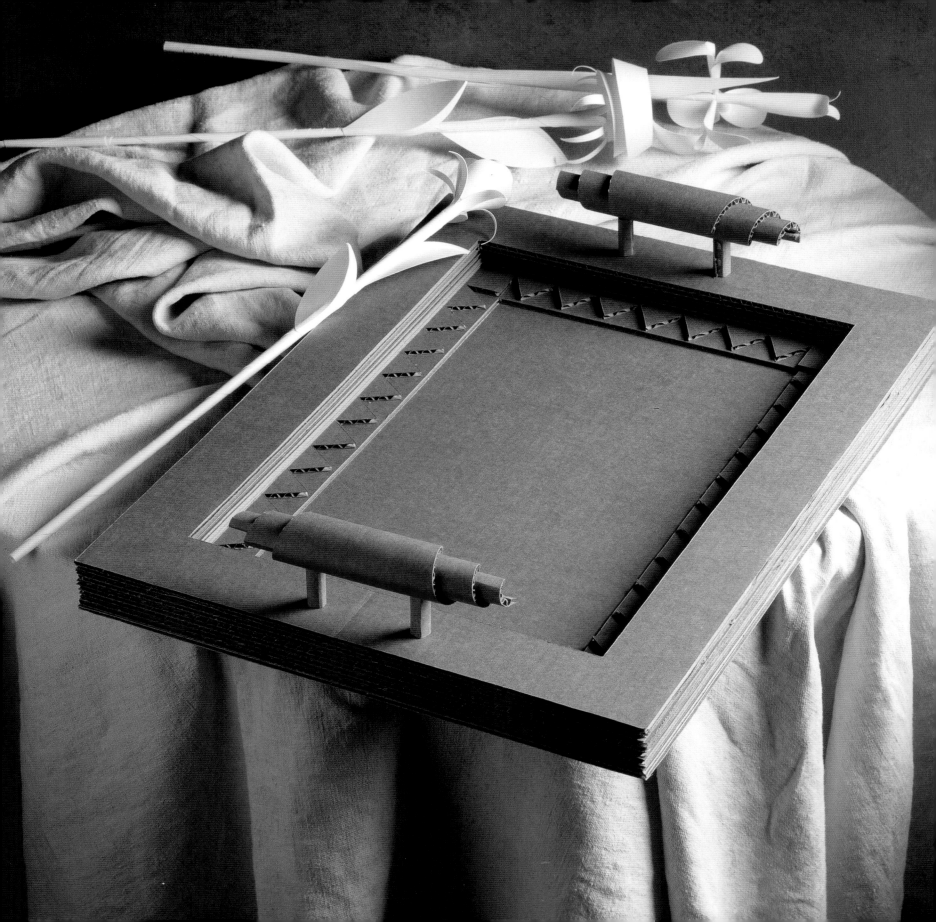

# WALL SCONCE

THIS ELEGANT WALL SCONCE LOOKS LIKE AN OLYMPIC TORCH WITH ITS CORRUGATED CONE AND CARDBOARD FLAMES. MAKE A PAIR OF THEM AND DISPLAY ONE ON EITHER SIDE OF A PAINTING OR ILLUMINATE YOUR HALLWAY.

A SMALL METAL PÂTISSERIE TIN IS USED AS THE CANDLE HOLDER. AS A SAFETY PRECAUTION, THE SCONCE MUST BE SPRAYED WITH A NON-FLAMMABLE SPRAY BEFORE USE. USE TALL CANDLES AND NEVER LEAVE THEM UNATTENDED WHEN THEY ARE LIT.

**1** Trace the oval template from the back of the book and enlarge to size. Cut out one oval from single wall cardboard measuring 18 cm/7 in at the longest length, and one smaller oval measuring 10 cm/4 in at its longest length. For each oval, cut out three slightly larger pieces of cardboard. Stick one of the ovals on to one piece of cardboard and cut round it. Repeat with the two remaining pieces. Do the same with the other oval. (Each oval now has four layers of cardboard.)

**2** Measure and cut out a piece of cardboard 25 cm x 11 cm/10 in x 4½ in, with the shortest edge running along the grooves. Peel the back off either by gently pulling it away or by cutting it in strips if it is very tough (see Basic Techniques). Cut two smaller strips of corrugated packing cardboard measuring 12 cm x 2 cm/4¾ in x ¾ in wide.

**3** Spread glue over the corrugated side of the rectangle of cardboard and roll it up tightly. Hold it in place until the glue has dried. Put glue on the flat side of the two smaller strips and glue them on to the ends of the roll. Glue the small oval of cardboard in the middle of the large one. ▶

## MATERIALS AND EQUIPMENT YOU WILL NEED

TRACING PAPER • PENCIL • SINGLE WALL CORRUGATED CARDBOARD • CRAFT KNIFE • CUTTING MAT • METAL RULER • HIGH-TACK GLUE •
SINGLE-FACED CORRUGATED PACKING CARDBOARD • PAIR OF COMPASSES • SMALL METAL PÂTISSERIE TIN • NON-FLAMMABLE SPRAY • PLATE HOOK DISK

4 Put glue on one end of the roll of cardboard and stick it on to the middle of the small oval. Apply plenty of glue because the adhesion needs to be fairly strong. Using a pair of compasses, draw a circle on to a piece of single wall cardboard with a radius of 2.5 cm/1 in. Cut it out, stick it on to another piece of cardboard and cut out so that the circle is two layers thick. Glue on to the end of the roll.

6 Starting from the longest length, roll up the triangle, applying blobs of glue every so often and finishing by gluing the end in place. Be careful not to squash the cardboard as you roll it. Gently reshape any grooves that are slightly flat.

8 Trace the flame-shaped templates from the back of the book, enlarging to size, and cut out five of the larger shaped flames and five of the smaller shapes from packing cardboard. Draw the shapes on the flat side and cut out with a craft knife, ensuring that it is very sharp. Glue the large flame shapes around the pâtisserie tin.

5 On the smooth side of a large piece of packing cardboard, draw a right-angled triangle 54 cm/21½ in wide and 29 cm/11½ in long. Cut it out with a very sharp craft knife. Packing cardboard tends to tear if the blade is not sharp.

7 Stick the rolled cone on to the circle on the end of the roll (see step 4). Cut out a circle with a radius of 2 cm/¾ in, one with a radius of 2.5 cm/1 in and another one with a radius of 4 cm/1½ in. Using the method from step 1, make the two smaller circles two layers of cardboard thick and the largest circle four layers thick. Glue them all centrally on top of each other in graduating sizes and stick on to the cone.

9 Continue to stick the flame shapes on to the dish, sticking the smaller shapes between the large shapes. Glue the dish on to the sconce and gently bend the flames so that they are slightly curved away from where the candle will sit. Cut a strip of packing cardboard 15 cm x 1 cm/6 in x ½ in and glue it around the base of the pâtisserie tin and flames. Spray the whole sconce with a non-flammable spray. Glue a plate hook disk on to the back for hanging.

# WALL BRACKET

ADD A TOUCH OF FOLLY TO A ROOM WITH THIS CARDBOARD WALL BRACKET. THE WHITE-PAINTED DESIGN EMULATES OLD PLASTERWORK AND THE TRADITIONAL ACANTHUS LEAVES GIVE IT A CLASSICAL LOOK. THE WALL BRACKET COULD BE LEFT IN ITS NATURAL CARDBOARD FINISH FOR A CONTEMPORARY LOOK, OR PAINTED TO MATCH THE COLOUR OF THE WALL WHERE IT WILL HANG. USE IT TO DISPLAY A VASE (CHECK THAT IT IS STRONG ENOUGH) OR TO HOLD POSTCARDS OR PHOTOGRAPHS. IT WILL LOOK ESPECIALLY GOOD IN A ROOM WHERE THE ORIGINAL PLASTERWORK FEATURES HAVE BEEN RETAINED.

1 Measure and cut out two rectangles of double wall cardboard 20 cm x 16 cm/ 8 in x 6¼ in. Glue them together. Cut out two rectangles measuring 18 cm x 20 cm/ 7 in x 8 in and glue them together.

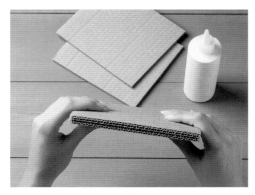

2 From the same cardboard, cut out two rectangles measuring 14 cm x 17 cm/ 5½ in x 6¾ in and two more 15 cm x 17 cm/ 6 in x 6¾ in. Glue them together.

3 Take the two larger pieces of double wall cardboard from step 1. Apply glue to the longer edge of the smaller piece and place it flat on the work surface. Ensuring that it is the right way round, press the other piece at right angles against the glued end and hold it in place firmly until it is dry. Do the same with the two smaller pieces of double wall cardboard then glue these inside the larger bracket.

4 From the corrugated packing cardboard, cut out a rectangle measuring 100 cm x 30 cm/40 in x 12 in. Draw a line on the corrugated side 7.5 cm/3 in from both long edges using a ruler. Carefully score along the line with a craft knife, taking care not to cut into the cardboard.

▶

## MATERIALS AND EQUIPMENT YOU WILL NEED

DOUBLE WALL MEDIUM FLUTE CORRUGATED CARDBOARD • CRAFT KNIFE • CUTTING MAT • GLUE • SINGLE-FACED CORRUGATED PACKING CARDBOARD •

PENCIL • METAL RULER • TRACING PAPER • SCISSORS • WATER-BASED WHITE PAINT • PAINTBRUSH • PLATE HOOK DISK

5 Fold the packing cardboard over along the score lines with the corrugated sides together. Roll it up loosely from one end, with the join on the inside, to form a large roll. Turn the cardboard over and roll from the other end to form a scroll shape. Glue both rolls in place.

6 When the glue is dry and the scroll stuck firmly, apply glue along the top and back of the scroll and fix it in position on the bracket. Leave to dry.

7 Cut strips of packing cardboard about 1 cm/½ in wide and long enough to fit right round the scroll. Glue the corrugated sides, stick them on to the scroll about 2 cm/¾ in from the edge. Cut a smaller strip about 4 cm/1½ in wide and stick it over the join on the lower part of the scroll, then stick a strip of 1 cm/½ in wide cardboard, corrugated side up, down the middle of that.

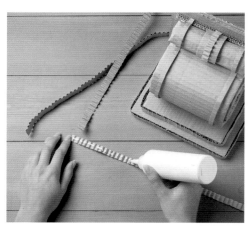

8 Cut long strips of packing cardboard wide enough to cover the edges of the bracket and glue in place. Stick the strips around the edge of the large outer bracket and along the edge of the smaller inner bracket. Hold them in place to ensure a good adhesion.

9 Trace the template from the back of the book and enlarge it, then cut out the acanthus leaves in four different sizes. Draw round the shapes on to the flat side of the packing cardboard and cut them out with scissors. Cut a strip of card, about 17 cm/6¾ in long and 2 cm/¾ in wide at one end, tapering to 1 cm/½ in wide at the other.

10 Glue the leaves in place on to the scroll, smallest at the top, overlapping them slightly so that they curl upwards. Glue the tapered strip down the middle. When the glue is dry, paint the bracket with white paint, dabbing the brush inside the scroll and behind the leaves so that no plain cardboard is visible. Glue a plate hook disk on to the back.

# CARD TABLE

THE INGENIOUS CONSTRUCTION OF THIS TABLE MEANS THAT IT IS NOT ONLY A VERY STRONG, STURDY PIECE OF FURNITURE, BUT DUAL PURPOSE AS WELL. SWIVEL THE TOP ROUND AND OPEN IT OUT TO USE IT AS A CARD TABLE OR KEEP IT FOLDED AS A SIDE TABLE. THE TABLE ILLUSTRATES THE DURABILITY OF CARDBOARD AND SHOWS THAT IT REALLY CAN BE USED FOR SO MANY THINGS WHEN THE CONSTRUCTION IS CAREFULLY THOUGHT OUT. WHEN PUTTING THE TABLE TOGETHER, WORK ON A VERY FLAT, SOLID SURFACE TO ENSURE THAT THE LEGS AND RAILS ARE ALL LEVEL SO THAT THE TABLE WILL NOT WOBBLE.

1 Following diagram A at the back of the book, draw and cut out four leg pieces from cardboard. Using the wooden spoon and wooden ruler, score along the fold lines. Press down firmly, being careful not to rip the cardboard.

2 Carefully fold the cardboard along the lines, gently easing it into place. Lift and fold the central line away from the surface and fold the lines on either side the other way so that the cardboard concertinas slightly.

3 Fold the cardboard right over so that the two flat edges meet. Apply wood glue to one side and press them together firmly.

## MATERIALS AND EQUIPMENT YOU WILL NEED

TRACING PAPER • PENCIL • DOUBLE WALL CORRUGATED CARDBOARD • METAL RULER • HEAVY-DUTY CRAFT KNIFE • CUTTING MAT • WOODEN SPOON • WOODEN RULER •
WOOD GLUE • ELASTIC BANDS • CLOTHES PEGS • PLASTIC OVERFLOW TANK COUPLER (2 CM/¾ IN) • HACKSAW • SCISSORS • FELT • PVA GLUE

4 Put elastic bands around the whole leg to hold it in place and peg the glued flaps together with a clothes peg. Leave to dry completely. Repeat with the remaining three legs. Remove the pegs and elastic bands.

5 Using diagrams B and C as a guide, cut out four side rails – two long and two short. Score along the fold lines with the wooden spoon on all four pieces.

6 Carefully fold the cardboard along the long scored lines until the side flaps meet. Apply plenty of wood glue to one side and sandwich the rail together.

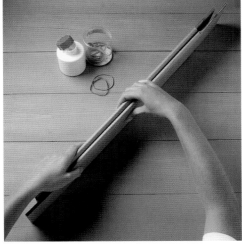

7 Put elastic bands around the rail until it is completely dry. Repeat with the remaining three rail pieces. Remove the elastic bands when the glue is dry.

8 Following diagram D, cut out a piece of cardboard for the cross rail. As before, score along the fold lines and fold the longest lines over. Stick in place with wood glue and secure with elastic bands until dry. Remove the elastic bands and fold the end flaps over.

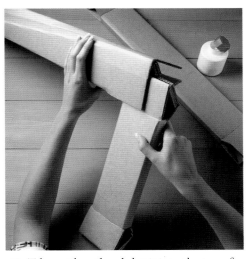

9 Take a side rail and slot it into the top of one of the legs of the table. Bend the longest flap over at each end of the rail so that it forms a triangle with the other smaller flap. When you are sure that the rail piece fits well into the leg, glue it in place.

10 Slot the other side rail pieces into the legs, again making sure that they fit well before gluing in place. Make sure that all the rails are the right way up. The single fold should be at the top. ▶

**11** Take the cross rail and slot it between the two long rails as shown in diagram G. It should be a snug fit. Glue in position and then leave to dry completely.

**12** Cut out a rectangle of cardboard 130 cm x 100 cm/51 in x 40 in and two pieces 75 cm x 100 cm/30 in x 40 in for the table top (see diagrams E and F). Measure and draw a line 10 cm/4 in from the edge all the way round on each piece. Mitre the corners so that when they are folded over the corners will fit neatly together. Score along the pencil lines with the wooden spoon. Fold the flaps inwards, and cut out a rectangle of cardboard to fit inside the central area. Repeat for each piece of the table top, but for the larger rectangle cut it in half. Stick the rectangles in place then glue down the flaps. Weigh down the corners with weights or pans of water until the glue is dry.

**13** Next, mark the position of the swivel joint (the overflow coupler) on one of the smaller pieces of the table top. Measure 21 cm/8¼ in from one end of the inset rectangle and 8 cm/3 in from the longest edge. Saw the overflow coupler in half and draw around the widest part. Cut out a hole in the inset layer of cardboard. Cut a smaller hole (wide enough for the thread of the coupler to fit through) in the other layer of cardboard. Insert the coupler.

**14** Place the large piece on the work surface, mitred side up, and apply glue liberally all over it. Stick the two smaller pieces on top, lining up the corners. Put weights on top while it dries.

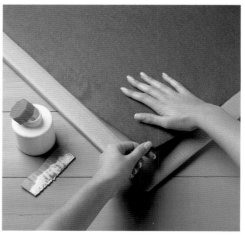

**15** Cut out a piece of felt and stick it on to the solid side of the cardboard table top with PVA glue. Press it down well and smooth out any air bubbles with the palm of your hand. When the glue is dry, fold the table top in half and bolt the top on to the base using the coupler. To open the table out, turn it to open it up, so that it lies flat on the base.

**16** Cut a hole in the crossrail to take the coupler in diagram E. Lay the table top on the surface crossrail with the coupler sticking up. Push the coupler through the hole in the cross rail, put the washer on top and screw the nut on tightly.

# CHEST OF DRAWERS

THIS CHEST OF DRAWERS IS MADE FROM CHILDREN'S SHOE BOXES PAINTED IN LOVELY BRIGHT COLOURS, SO IT WILL APPEAL TO CHILDREN OF ANY AGE. IT CAN BE MADE BIGGER USING LARGER SHOE BOXES AND IS IDEAL FOR STORING STATIONERY, SEWING TOOLS AND BITS AND BOBS AS WELL AS CHILDREN'S THINGS. FOR A FINAL DECORATIVE TOUCH, PAINTED WOODEN HANDLES OR TASSELS LOOK GREAT AND KNOTS OF COLOURFUL CORD COULD ALSO BE USED TO EMBELLISH THE BOXES.

**1** Measure the height and width of one box and multiply both measurements by three, then measure the length of one box, and add 1 cm/½ in to each of these three measurements. Cut eight pieces of polyboard: two for the top and base, which are the length by the width plus the thickness of four pieces of polyboard; two for the horizontal struts, which are the length by the width plus the thickness of two pieces of polyboard; and four for the vertical struts, which are the length by the height plus the thickness of two widths of polyboard. Cut slits wide enough to take the thickness of one piece of polyboard a third and two thirds of the way along two of the horizontal struts and two of the vertical struts.

**2** Slot the pieces of polyboard together at right angles as shown. Put to one side.

**3** Lay one of the pieces of polyboard you cut for the top and base on the work surface. This will be the base. Glue the two remaining vertical struts at right angles at either end of the base. Pin them in place to secure. When the glue has dried, glue the top pieces, pinning them in place. Leave to dry. ▶

MATERIALS AND EQUIPMENT YOU WILL NEED

NINE SHOE BOXES • METAL RULER • POLYBOARD • PENCIL • CRAFT KNIFE • CUTTING MAT • WOOD GLUE • DRESSMAKER'S PINS • WATER-BASED PAINTS IN THREE COLOURS • PAINTBRUSH • NINE WOODEN KNOBS AND SCREWS • BRADAWL • SCREWDRIVER • SINGLE WALL CORRUGATED PACKING CARDBOARD

4 Lay the open box shape on the work surface. Apply glue to all the ends of the polyboard grid and place it inside the box. Pin from the outside through the polyboard so that it is securely fixed together. Cut a piece of polyboard the width and height of the whole box and glue and pin it to the back of the frame.

5 Paint the shoe boxes with one of the water-based paints. Paint the lid as well. The inside of the boxes could be painted with a co-ordinating paint or lined with patterned wrapping paper if desired. You may need to give them two coats of paint for an even coverage. Paint the chest in another colour and leave to dry.

6 Paint the wooden handles with the same colour of paint as the chest. When the paint on the boxes and the handles is dry, make a hole with a bradawl in the front of each box. Fix a handle to each box front.

7 Cut a long piece of corrugated packing cardboard the width of the chest and long enough to make a scroll shape for the feet. Roll it up from both ends until the rolls are the required size and equal to each other. Glue in place.

8 Cut another strip of corrugated packing cardboard the same width and long enough to cover the top of the chest in a wavy shape. Paint the long strip and the rolls with the third paint colour.

9 Stick the long strip up the side of the chest, turning the edge under the bottom of the chest, and glue in three waves across the top. Glue down the other side and leave to dry. Pin in place down the sides.

10 Apply glue to the top of each roll and centre the chest on top. Leave to dry.

# SATCHEL

THIS SATCHEL HARDLY LOOKS LIKE CARDBOARD AT ALL. IT MAKES CLEVER USE OF THE WAX USED TO WATERPROOF CLOTHING, WHICH NOT ONLY MAKES THE BAG MORE PRACTICAL BUT ADDS A LOVELY MOTTLED PATINA TO THE MATERIAL. THE SATCHEL IS BOUND WITH PAPER STRING IN KEEPING WITH THE CARDBOARD THEME AND THE BINDING MAKES FOR A VERY STURDY, ROBUST RESULT.

AS A CONTRAST TO THE PLAIN CARDBOARD, THE BAG CAN BE LINED WITH WALLPAPER AS IT HAS BEEN HERE, OR WITH PATTERNED FABRIC TO GIVE A NICE FINISH INSIDE. IT IS MADE IN THE STYLE OF A TRADITIONAL SCHOOL SATCHEL BUT IT IS SMART ENOUGH FOR AN OFFICE, AND YOU COULD ADD A LONGER PLAITED STRING HANDLE TO CREATE A SHOULDER BAG.

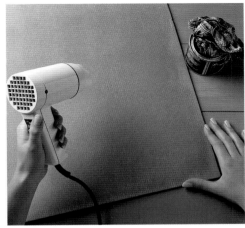

1 Spray adhesive on to the back of the wallpaper and stick it on to one side of the corrugated cardboard. Start from one edge and gently wipe over the wallpaper to achieve a smooth finish free of air bubbles.

2 Using a soft cloth, apply wax all over the other side of the card, ensuring that there is an even coverage. Using a hairdryer, melt the wax so it soaks in and is less greasy.

3 Using the diagram at the back of the book, cut out piece A which is the back and front flap. Score the lines with the blunt point of a wooden spoon (see Basic Techniques). Do not use a craft knife as this will cut into the wallpaper. Cut small holes for the eyelets and insert eyelets. Cut out the oval holes for the fastenings on the front flap. Punch holes all around the outside, 1.5cm/⅝ in apart. ▶

MATERIALS AND EQUIPMENT YOU WILL NEED

WALLPAPER • SPRAY ADHESIVE • SMALL FLUTE SINGLE WALL CORRUGATED CARDBOARD • SOFT CLOTH • WAX FOR WATERPROOF CLOTHING •
HAIRDRYER • TRACING PAPER • PENCIL • CRAFT KNIFE • METAL RULER • CUTTING MAT • WOODEN SPOON •
EYELETS AND EYELET PUNCH • REVOLVING HOLE PUNCH • PAPER STRING • PLASTIC PIPING • METAL FASTENERS AND WASHERS

4 Cut out the outside front (B), two side pieces for the pocket (D), two side pieces for the satchel pocket (C) and the pocket front (E) from the wallpapered cardboard. Also cut out the inside pocket divider (F), which should be papered on both sides. Punch holes 1.5 cm/⅝ in apart along three sides, leaving the top edge free.

6 Score along all the fold lines on the two side pieces (C) and bend along all the lines. Stitch one of them around the back satchel piece (A) and continue threading the string through all the holes on the flap. Lay the inside pocket divider (F) on top of this and lay the second side piece (D) on top. Stitch through all the layers.

8 Cut out a handle (G) and fold along the lines as indicated. Punch holes 1.5 cm/⅝ in apart along the longest sides. Thread a double thickness of string through both of the eyelet holes and tie with a knot. Wrap the cardboard handle around the string and stitch together. (It is a good idea to use a piece of plastic piping to reinforce the handle.)

5 On the unprepared side of the side piece for the pocket (D), score along the fold lines, then make the folds. Centre the pocket (E) on the satchel front (B) and mark the position. Put the pocket (E) to one side. Position the pocket side (D) along the marked line, then punch matching holes in the two layers of cardboard and stitch on to the front of the satchel by threading the string through the holes, starting and ending with a knot on the papered side. Fold over 2 cm/¾ in along the straight edge of the pocket front (E) and attach to the pocket side (D).

7 Hold the front of the satchel (B) in place against the side strip (C). Stitch in place with the string, finishing by threading the string back through the previous hole and tying a knot inside.

9 Hold the front flap flat against the satchel. Using a pencil, mark the positions for the backs of the fastenings on the pocket front. Carefully push the backs of the metal fasteners through the cardboard. Bolt the other parts of the fasteners in the position marked. Use washers to stop them cutting through the cardboard.

# CHRISTMAS TREE DECORATIONS

THESE DELICATE DECORATIONS STARTED LIFE AS THE CARDBOARD BACKING ON ENVELOPES, WHICH MAKES THEM VERY ECONOMICAL AND AN ELEGANT WAY TO RECYCLE! THEY ARE CONSTRUCTED FROM TWO PIECES OF ORNATELY SHAPED CARDBOARD SLOTTED TOGETHER AND DECORATED WITH BEAUTIFUL BEADS. YOU COULD MAKE THEM IN DIFFERENT SIZES AND HANG THEM ON THE CHRISTMAS TREE, OR DISPLAY THEM IN A WINDOW BY HANGING THEM FROM RIBBONS OF DIFFERENT LENGTHS.

**1** Trace the templates from the back of the book. Draw around them on to the card, drawing two pieces for each decoration. Cut out each shape using small scissors (such as embroidery scissors) or a craft knife.

**2** Mark the slotting slits down the centre of both pieces and cut them out with a craft knife, metal ruler and cutting mat. Do not overcut the slits or the shapes will not hold together tightly.

**3** Using a bradawl, make a small hole close to the bottom edge of one piece for the central bead drop, a hole at the top of the corresponding piece for the hanging loop, and holes close to the edges underneath the top curling shapes to hang more beads.

**4** Thread the beads on to flat-headed pins to make the droplets, one for the base centre and one for each of the four top curls.

**5** Using long-nosed pliers, bend each wire close to the top of the beads and hook through a hole in the card. Wrap the wire ends around the pin a few times to secure, and trim the ends.

**6** Slot the two beaded card pieces together until they match at top and bottom edges, to make a three-dimensional shape. Thread a piece of cord through the top hole and tie the ends to make a hanging loop. Trim the excess cord.

## MATERIALS AND EQUIPMENT YOU WILL NEED

TRACING PAPER • PENCIL • MEDIUM-WEIGHT MANILA CARD • PENCIL • SMALL SCISSORS (OPTIONAL) • CRAFT KNIFE • METAL RULER •
CUTTING MAT • BRADAWL • BEADS • FLAT-HEADED PINS • LONG-NOSED PLIERS • THIN CORD

# WOVEN BASKET

THIS BASKET IS AN INGENIOUS WAY OF USING FOOD PACKAGING BOXES. IT USES A TRADITIONAL WEAVING TECHNIQUE WHICH CREATES A ROBUST BASKET THAT IS HARDLY RECOGNIZABLE AS CARDBOARD AT ALL. IT HAS BEEN GIVEN A MODERN LOOK BY PAINTING IT IN BRIGHT COLOURS WITH A SIMPLE PATTERN THAT IS EASY TO DO. THE CONSTRUCTION MAKES IT STRONG ENOUGH TO USE AS A SHOPPING BASKET AND IT WOULD LOOK GREAT FULL OF FRUIT AND VEG FROM THE MARKET.

THE EYELET AND ROPE CAN BE BOUGHT FROM BOATING SHOPS AND THE REVOLVING HOLE PUNCH IS A VERY HANDY TOOL, AVAILABLE FROM HARDWARE STORES, WHICH IS WELL WORTH INVESTING IN IF YOU PLAN TO MAKE WOVEN-CARDBOARD BASKETS.

1 Open out the cardboard boxes into large sheets and paint with a bold random pattern. Leave to dry. On the unpainted side, rule into 4 cm/1½ in wide strips – rule across the corrugations, not along them – in the following lengths: three x 110 cm/43 in, nine x 80 cm/32 in, eight x 120 cm/47 in and two extra x 120 cm/47 in (for spares).

2 Using a pair of scissors, cut up the strips of cardboard.

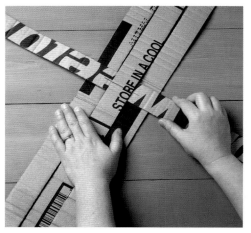

3 Take the three 110 cm/43 in strips and make a mark across the middle of all three strips. Take one 80 cm/32 in strip and make a mark along the middle of the strip at a central point. With the paint side down, lay out the three long strips, lining up the marks. Lift up the middle strip, and lay one of the 80 cm/32 in strips across and on top of the remaining two 110 cm/43 in strips, using the marks to line up the strips. This is the first woven strip and should travel over, under, then over the other three.

## MATERIALS AND EQUIPMENT YOU WILL NEED

TWO OR THREE CARDBOARD BOXES • PVA PAINT IN SEVERAL COLOURS • PAINTBRUSH • METAL RULER • PENCIL •
SCISSORS • 20–30 HINGED CLOTHES PEGS • STRONG THREAD • SHARP NEEDLE WITH LARGE EYE • BODKIN • STRONG, QUICK-DRYING GLUE •
HOLE-MAKING TOOL • FOUR 1 CM/½ IN BRASS EYELETS AND "PUNCH AND DIE" KIT • BRIGHTLY COLOURED POLYPROPYLENE STRING •
MATT POLYURETHANE VARNISH • PAINTBRUSH • 1.5–2 M/60–80 IN OF 1 CM/½ IN DIAMETER ROPE • MASKING TAPE

4 Beginning on one side of the single strip, fold the two outer strips tightly up over the central strip. Lay a second strip on top of the middle of the three 110 cm / 32 in strips, as close as possible to the first woven strip. Line up the ends of the strips.

5 Fold the two outer strips back down so that they lie as smoothly as possible over the second woven strip. Fold the central 110 cm / 43 in strip tightly up over the two woven strips. Lay a third strip on top of the two outer 110 cm / 43 in strips, as close as possible to the first two woven strips.

6 Continue until there are five 80 cm / 32 in strips woven through the three 110 cm / 43 in strips. Peg the two corners, turn the work around then weave the remaining four 80 cm / 32 in strips on the other side of the central 80 cm / 32 in strip. Peg the corners. Check that every strip has travelled "over one, under one" to give a chequered effect.

7 Bend up the strips around the edge of the woven base – these will now be called the side stakes. Take one of the 120 cm / 47 in strips and, starting just to one side of the centre of a long edge, place the end of the strip between two of the side strips, maintaining the "over one, under one" weave pattern up the sides. Check that this pattern will continue when deciding where to place the first 120 cm / 47 in weaving strip. Begin working around the base, folding the side strips from the inside tightly down over the weaving strip, and those from the outside tightly to the inside. Peg the strips that fold to the outside.

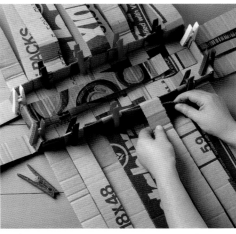

8 Make sure the weaving strip closely follows the line of the edge of the base – there should be no gaps between the base and the sides. Aim to get sharp corners, as this will influence the shape of the finished basket.

9 At the end of this (and each following) row, overlap the ends of the weaving strip, so that it runs in a double layer across three or four of the side strips. Begin the second row as the first, but on the opposite long edge. Remember to check that the "over one, under one" weave pattern is continued. ▶

**10** Work six rows, beginning each row on alternate sides. Measure a length of thread that goes easily twice around the basket. With the side stakes upright and using a bodkin, stitch around the top row of weaving to secure it. Using scissors, trim off the excess side strips slightly below the top edge of the final row.

**12** Using a hole-making tool, make two clean holes for the brass eyelets in each long side of the basket. These should be three "squares" in from the outer edge, in the row below the border strip (there will be three "squares" between the holes). Mark the positions of the holes first to check they are in the correct place.

**14** Measure a length of coloured string that goes easily three and a half times around the basket. Work blanket stitch around the border strips, spacing the stitches 4 cm/1½ in apart to correspond to the width of the cardboard strips. If necessary, enlarge the stitching holes with a bodkin. Keep the stitching tight and even. Varnish the basket inside and out to protect it.

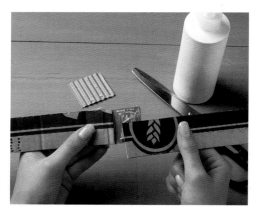

**11** Take one of the remaining 120 cm/ 47 in strips (a border strip), glue the back and stick it to the inside of the top row of the basket. Use clothes pegs to hold the strip in place, and to create sharp creases at the corner points. Overlap the ends (see Basic Techniques). Glue the back of the other border strip and stick it to the outside of the top row, again using pegs to hold it in place until the glue is completely dry, and making sure the corners are sharp.

**13** Insert and secure the brass eyelets using the punch and die, following the instructions on the packet.

**15** Cut the rope in half, taping the ends to stop them fraying. Make a knot at one end. Thread the rope through the first eyelet hole from inside to outside, leaving the knot on the inside of the basket. Thread the other end of the rope through the second eyelet hole from outside to inside, then make a knot in the other end of the rope. Repeat for the second handle, making sure the handles are the same length.

# CHILD'S CHAIR

THIS CHILD'S CHAIR IS MADE FROM DOUBLE WALL CORRUGATED CARDBOARD WHICH IS AVAILABLE IN LARGE SHEETS FROM PACKAGING AND BOX MANUFACTURERS. IT COULD BE MADE EVEN TOUGHER BY USING TRIPLE WALL CARDBOARD, ALTHOUGH THIS CAN BE DIFFICULT TO GET HOLD OF. THE CONSTRUCTION OF THE SEAT, BY FOLDING THE CARDBOARD INTO TRIANGLES, MAKES A STURDY BASE AND THE SHAPED BACK CREATES A MINIATURE THRONE. PAINTED COTTON MOULDS, WHICH ARE SOLD BY JEWELLERY SUPPLIERS, ARE STUCK ON TO THE POINTS OF THE CROWN SHAPE, BUT YOU COULD USE PING-PONG BALLS INSTEAD.

1 Cut a piece of cardboard 96 cm x 72 cm/ 40 in x 29 in for the back and sides. Draw a line 34 cm/13½ in from each side edge with the corrugated ridges running vertically (leaving a 28 cm/11 in wide centre panel).

2 Measure and draw a line 41 cm/16¼ in from the bottom edge across the two 34 cm/13½ in widths. Draw another line 6 cm/2½ in above that and another one 7 cm/2¾ in above that (see diagrams).

3 Make a paper template of a crown shape, then draw a crown shape on the back section of the chair (following the diagram at the back of the book). Line up the bottom of the template with the lines on either side of the central panel, tape in place and draw around with a pencil. Cut along the top line on either side of the chair and around the crown shape.

4 Measure and draw a faint line 10 cm/4 in long and 1 cm/½ in from the innermost line on either side of the chair back 25 cm/ 10 in from the bottom edge. Draw a horizontal line 10 cm/4 in long, 10 cm/4 in from the end of the first line. Mark the centre of these lines and with a set square, put a mark at right angles 9.5 cm/3¾ in from this. Join the marks together to form a triangle. Repeat this on either side of the chair. ▶

## MATERIALS AND EQUIPMENT YOU WILL NEED

DOUBLE WALL CORRUGATED CARDBOARD • HEAVY-DUTY CRAFT KNIFE • METAL RULER • PENCIL • CUTTING MAT • TRACING PAPER • MASKING TAPE • SET SQUARE • SMALL PAINT CAN OR PLATE • WOODEN SPOON • GLUE GUN • STRONG GLUE • THREE COTTON MOULDS • PAINT • PAINTBRUSH

**5** Cut out the triangles using the craft knife and metal ruler. Take a small paint can or plate and use it to draw a curve on the arm of the chair. Draw a line from the edge of the curve vertically to the edge of the cardboard on the outermost panel. Cut around the curve and along the line.

**6** To make the seat, draw a rectangle measuring 28 cm x 70 cm/11 in x 27½ in in the centre of a piece of cardboard, with the longest length cutting across the corrugated ridges. Draw two lines 10 cm/4 in apart from each other at both ends of the rectangle. Measure and put a pencil mark 5.5 cm/2¼ in from the corners at one end of the rectangle. Mark 4 cm/1½ in out from the second line along and 7 cm/2¾ in out from the next line along. Draw lines joining the marks up.

**7** Measure and mark 5.5 cm/2¼ in from the other end of the rectangle. Join the end of the first line up with these marks. Repeat on both sides of the rectangle.

**8** Put marks 10 cm/4 in from the outside lines of the centre rectangle and draw a line from these marks 10 cm/4 in vertically. Join the bottom of the two lines together with a pencil line. Cut out the middle section.

**9** Take the back piece of the chair again. Using a wooden spoon or anything with a blunt point on it, score along the two lines that form the arms. Press down firmly, but ensure that the surface is just flattened slightly and not broken. Score the arm lines and fold over.

**10** Score along the lines on the seat by running the edge of your thumb along the lines between the grooves of the corrugated cardboard. Bend the cardboard along the score lines.

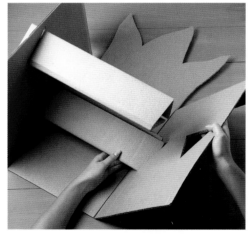

**11** Bend the back of the chair along the score lines and carefully slot one side of the seat into the cut-out triangles. Gently ease the other side of the seat into the triangles on the other side. The side piece may need to be bent very gently to slot it in, but be careful not to bend it too much. Glue along the edge of the arms with strong glue and fold it over and stick it on to the side of the chair. Paint the cotton moulds and glue them on to the points of the crown shape.

# TEMPLATES

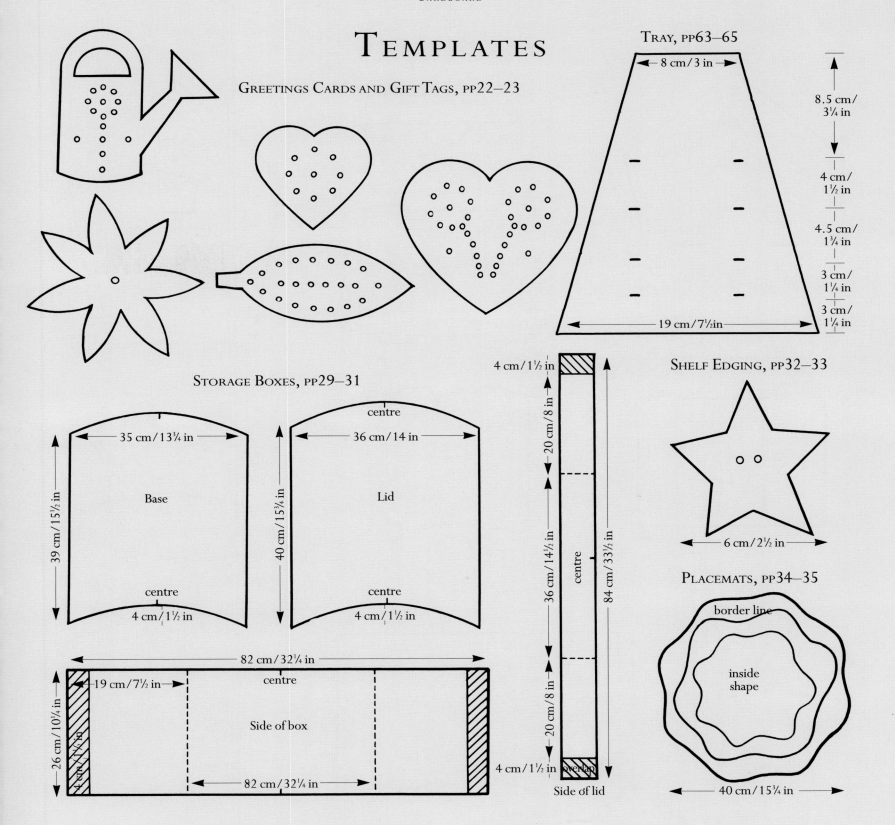

GREETINGS CARDS AND GIFT TAGS, pp22–23

TRAY, pp63–65

8 cm/3 in

8.5 cm/ 3¼ in

4 cm/ 1½ in

4.5 cm/ 1¾ in

3 cm/ 1¼ in

3 cm/ 1¼ in

19 cm/7½in

STORAGE BOXES, pp29–31

35 cm/13¾ in

Base

39 cm/15½ in

centre

4 cm/1½ in

centre

36 cm/14 in

Lid

40 cm/15¾ in

centre

4 cm/1½ in

82 cm/32¼ in

19 cm/7½ in

centre

Side of box

26 cm/10¼ in

82 cm/32¼ in

4 cm/1½ in

20 cm/8 in

centre

36 cm/14½ in

84 cm/33½ in

20 cm/8 in

4 cm/1½ in

overlap

Side of lid

SHELF EDGING, pp32–33

6 cm/2½ in

PLACEMATS, pp34–35

border line

inside shape

40 cm/15¾ in

# DOLL'S HOUSE, PP46–48

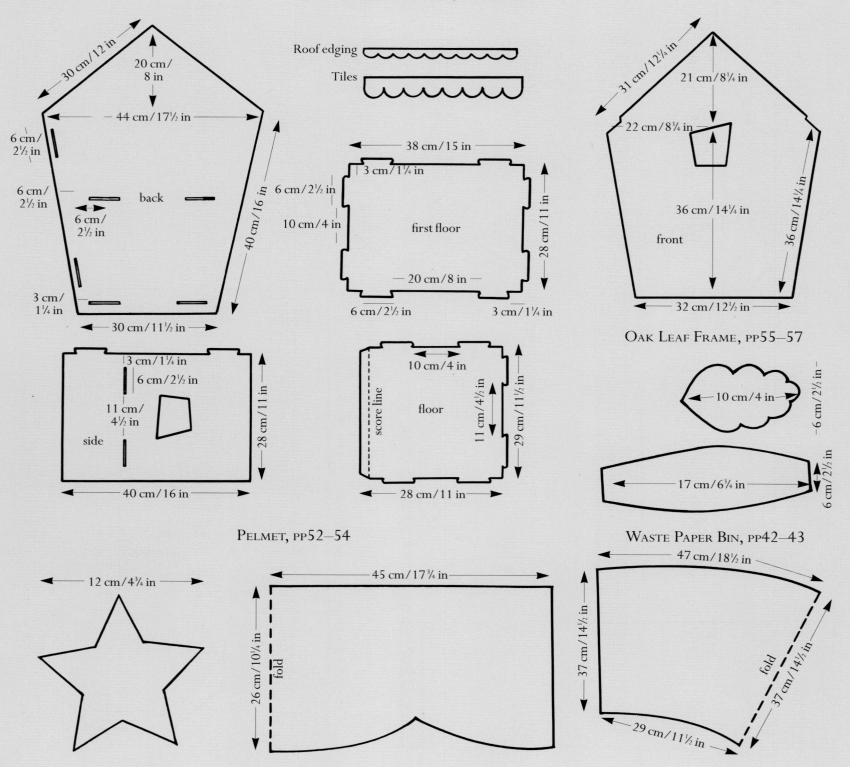

Roof edging

Tiles

30 cm/12 in
20 cm/8 in
44 cm/17½ in
6 cm/2½ in
6 cm/2½ in
back
6 cm/2½ in
40 cm/16 in
3 cm/1¼ in
30 cm/11½ in

38 cm/15 in
3 cm/1¼ in
6 cm/2½ in
first floor
10 cm/4 in
28 cm/11 in
20 cm/8 in
6 cm/2½ in
3 cm/1¼ in

31 cm/12¼ in
21 cm/8¼ in
22 cm/8¾ in
36 cm/14¼ in
front
36 cm/14¼ in
32 cm/12½ in

3 cm/1¼ in
6 cm/2½ in
11 cm/4½ in
side
28 cm/11 in
40 cm/16 in

10 cm/4 in
score line
floor
11 cm/4½ in
29 cm/11½ in
28 cm/11 in

## OAK LEAF FRAME, PP55–57

10 cm/4 in
6 cm/2½ in
17 cm/6¾ in
6 cm/2½ in
6 cm/2½ in

## PELMET, PP52–54

12 cm/4¾ in

45 cm/17¾ in
26 cm/10¼ in
fold

## WASTE PAPER BIN, PP42–43

47 cm/18½ in
37 cm/14½ in
fold
37 cm/14½ in
29 cm/11½ in

CARD TABLE, PP72–75

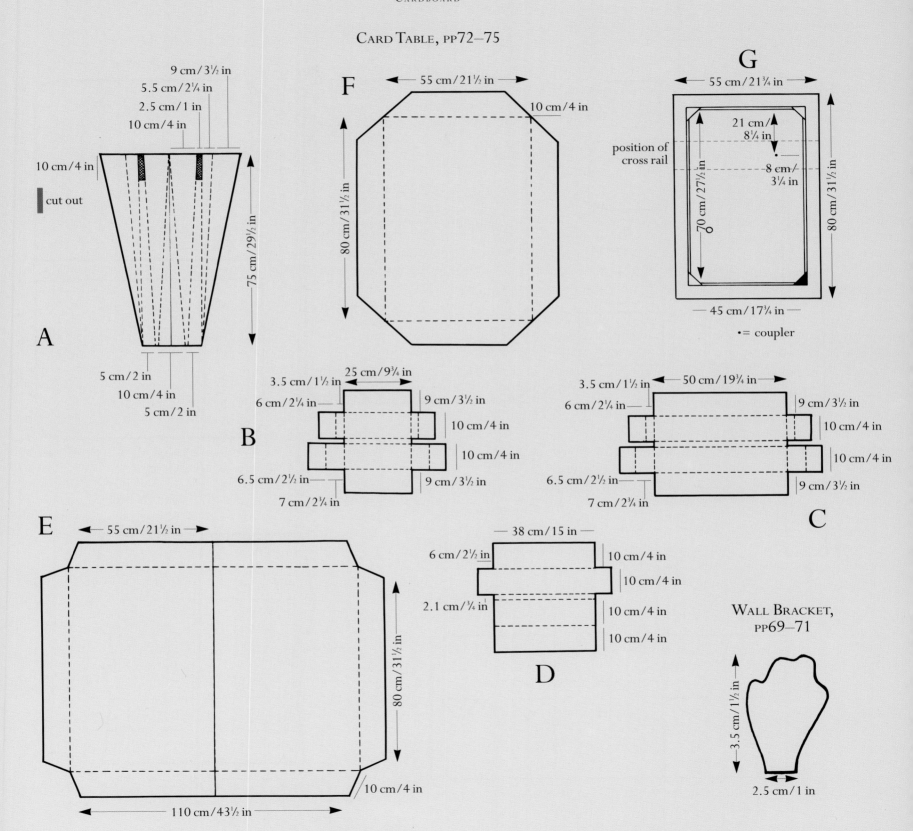

9 cm/3½ in
5.5 cm/2¼ in
2.5 cm/1 in
10 cm/4 in

10 cm/4 in

cut out

A

75 cm/29½ in

5 cm/2 in
10 cm/4 in
5 cm/2 in

F

← 55 cm/21½ in →

10 cm/4 in

80 cm/31½ in

G

← 55 cm/21¾ in →

position of
cross rail

21 cm/
8¼ in

8 cm/
3¼ in

70 cm/27½ in

80 cm/31½ in

— 45 cm/17¾ in —

•= coupler

B

3.5 cm/1½ in
6 cm/2¼ in

25 cm/9¾ in

9 cm/3½ in
10 cm/4 in
10 cm/4 in

6.5 cm/2½ in
7 cm/2¾ in

9 cm/3½ in

C

3.5 cm/1½ in
6 cm/2¼ in

50 cm/19¾ in

9 cm/3½ in
10 cm/4 in
10 cm/4 in

6.5 cm/2½ in
7 cm/2¾ in

9 cm/3½ in

E

← 55 cm/21½ in →

80 cm/31½ in

10 cm/4 in

← 110 cm/43½ in →

D

— 38 cm/15 in —

6 cm/2½ in
2.1 cm/¾ in

10 cm/4 in
10 cm/4 in
10 cm/4 in
10 cm/4 in

WALL BRACKET,
PP69–71

3.5 cm/1½ in

2.5 cm/1 in

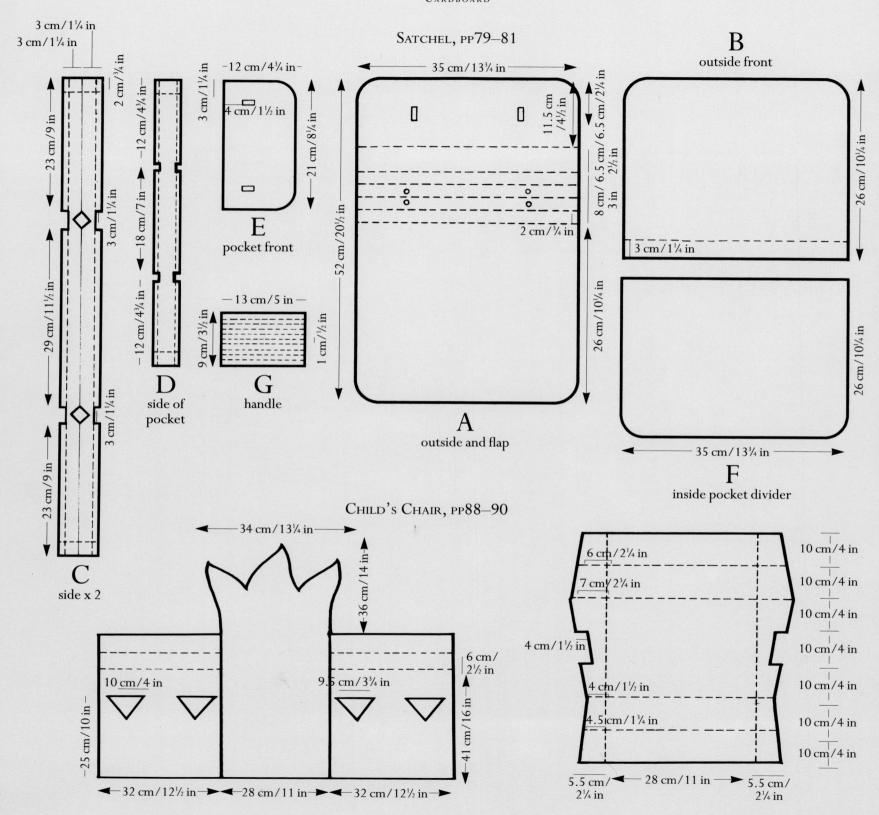

SATCHEL, PP79–81

B
outside front

3 cm/1¼ in
3 cm/1¼ in
2 cm/¾ in
23 cm/9 in
3 cm/1¼ in
29 cm/11½ in
3 cm/1¼ in
23 cm/9 in

C
side x 2

−12 cm/4¾ in−
−12 cm/4¾ in−
18 cm/7 in
−12 cm/4¾ in−

D
side of
pocket

−12 cm/4¾ in−
3 cm/1¼ in
4 cm/1½ in
21 cm/8¼ in

E
pocket front

−13 cm/5 in−
9 cm/3½ in
1 cm/½ in

G
handle

35 cm/13¾ in
11.5 cm/4½ in
8 cm/6.5 cm/6.5 cm/2¼ in
2½ in
3 in
2 cm/¾ in
52 cm/20½ in
26 cm/10¼ in

A
outside and flap

26 cm/10¼ in
3 cm/1¼ in

26 cm/10¼ in
35 cm/13¾ in

F
inside pocket divider

CHILD'S CHAIR, PP88–90

34 cm/13¼ in
36 cm/14 in
6 cm/2½ in
10 cm/4 in
9.5 cm/3¾ in
25 cm/10 in
41 cm/16 in
32 cm/12½ in
28 cm/11 in
32 cm/12½ in

6 cm/2¼ in
7 cm/2¾ in
4 cm/1½ in
4 cm/1½ in
4.5 cm/1¾ in
10 cm/4 in
10 cm/4 in
10 cm/4 in
10 cm/4 in
10 cm/4 in
10 cm/4 in
5.5 cm/2¼ in
28 cm/11 in
5.5 cm/2¼ in

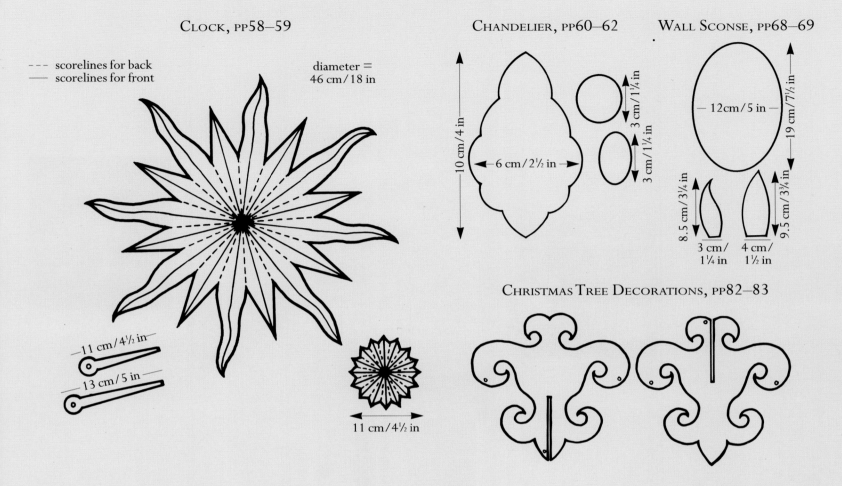

CLOCK, PP58–59

- - - scorelines for back
—— scorelines for front

diameter = 46 cm/18 in

11 cm/4½ in

13 cm/5 in

11 cm/4½ in

CHANDELIER, PP60–62

10 cm/4 in

6 cm/2½ in

3 cm/1¼ in

3 cm/1¼ in

WALL SCONCE, PP68–69

12cm/5 in

19 cm/7½ in

8.5 cm/3¼ in

9.5 cm/3¼ in

3 cm/ 1¼ in

4 cm/ 1½ in

CHRISTMAS TREE DECORATIONS, PP82–83

# SUPPLIERS AND ACKNOWLEDGEMENTS

Cardboard can be bought from many different shops and packaging suppliers. Craft and art shops and stationery stores sell a wide range of decorative card and cardboard in quite small quantities. For large amounts of heavy-duty cardboard, contact packaging companies. These should be listed in the telephone directory.

## ACKNOWLEDGEMENTS

The author and publishers would like to thank the following people who contributed projects to the book: Penny Boylan, pages 22, 24 and 44; Gloria Nicol, pages 29, 34 and 82; Andrew Gilmore, pages 72 and 79; Polly Pollock, page 84; and Mary Maguire, page 77. They would also like to thank the following people who lent items for the gallery: Tomoko Azumi (0171 435 5398); Carton Massif (items for sale at Interiors Bis, 60 Sloane Avenue, London SW3 3DD – 0171 838 1104); Sarah Drew, The Mount,

Pateley Bridge, Harrogate, Yorkshire HG3 5AP; Thomas Heatherwick, 129 Camden Mews, London NW1 9AH; Muji, 26 Great Marlborough Street, London W1( ring 0171 494 1197 for information of other shops); Polly Pollock, 221 Portobello Road, London W11; Lois Walpole, 100 Fairfoot Road, London E3 4EH; Nigel Westwood, 30 Trelawney Avenue, St Ives, Cornwall TR26 2AS.

## AUTHOR'S ACKNOWLEDGEMENTS

I would like to thank Peter Williams for his beautiful photography, Georgina Rhodes for her creative styling, Polly, Andrew, Mary, Gloria and Penny for their innovative projects and help with the research, and Clare Nicholson for her organization. A special thank you to Laurie for all his encouragement, and for never complaining about the amount of cardboard he was forced to live with.

# INDEX